NATURAL MAN

INTERIBERICA, S.A. DE EDICIONES

The Living Earth

NATURAL MAN

by Robert Allen

 The Danbury Press

A Division of Grolier Enterprises Inc.

THE DANBURY PRESS
A DIVISION OF GROLIER ENTERPRISES INC.

Publisher: ROBERT B. CLARKE

US ISBN: 0 7172 8104 3
Library of Congress Catalog Card No: 73 9922

© 1975 Interiberica, S.A. - Madrid
© 1973, © 1975 Aldus Books Limited, London

ISBN: 84-382-0012-5. Dep. Legal: M. 21.865-1975.

Printed and bound in Spain by Novograph
S.A., and Roner S.A., Crta de Irun, Km.12,450,
Madrid–34.

Series Coordinator	Geoffrey Rogers
Series Art Director	Frank Fry
Art Editor	Roger Hyde
Design Consultant	Guenther Radtke
Editorial Consultant	Malcolm Ross-Macdonald
Assistant Editors	Allyson Fawcett
	Bridget Gibbs
Copy Editor	Damian Grint
Research	Enid Moore
	Ann Fisher

Contents

From Apes to Man   8

!Kung Bushmen of the
Kalahari   16

Natural Man and his
Environment   36

Natural Man and his Fellows   78

Natural Man meets
Urban Man   118

Index   140

Editorial Advisers

MICHAEL BOORER, B.SC. Author, Lecturer, and Broadcaster.

MATTHEW BRENNAN, ED.D. Director, Brentree Environmental Center, Professor of Conservation Education, Pennsylvania State University.

PHYLLIS BUSCH, ED.D. Author, Science Teacher, and Consultant in Environmental Education.

KLAUS-FRIEDRICH KOCH. Assistant Professor of Social Anthropology, Harvard University.

VERNON REYNOLDS, B.A., M.A., PH.D. Lecturer in Physical Anthropology, Oxford University.

THE TWENTY VOLUMES IN THE LIVING EARTH SERIES

1	DESERT LIFE	11	RIVERS AND LAKES
2	FOREST LIFE	12	MOUNTAIN LIFE
3	NATURAL MAN	13	POLAR LIFE
4	EVERY LIVING THING	14	ISLAND LIFE
5	INVISIBLE WORLD	15	NATURE IN THE CITY
6	THE EARTH'S CRUST	16	WEB OF LIFE
7	THE AIR AROUND US	17	POLLUTION
8	WORLD OF PLANTS	18	CONSERVATION
9	GRASSLAND LIFE	19	LIFE IN THE FUTURE
10	SEAS AND OCEANS	20	GUIDE AND INDEX

Introduction

"It's not natural" is a common criticism of actions we dislike or do not understand. But how do we judge? In the sense that human beings are as much animals as are tigers or butterflies, all our actions are natural. At one time we regarded ourselves as morally superior to the other animals. But by studying animal behavior we have learned to marvel at the ability of other species to regulate their numbers, to ritualize and minimize violence, and so on, and now we consider man—potentially so violent, licentious, and greedy—as the most unnatural of animals.

Of course neither extreme is correct. Anthropologists have long recognized how misleading it is to use one cultural group—such as the people of the Western industrial countries—as the representatives of the whole of humanity. To look at natural man we must choose examples from those cultural types that have survived longest: the hunter-gatherers—peoples who live by hunting wild animals (including fish) and gathering wild plants. However, because societies that live substantially, though not completely, by food collecting often have similar characteristics to those that depend entirely on it, the term "natural man" refers not simply to pure hunter-gatherers but also to hunter-gardeners (people with a mixed food-collecting, food-cultivating economy).

From surviving and recently extinct hunting societies we can learn a great deal. They can help us answer some of the most vexing questions troubling us today. Are we innately violent and greedy? What do we mean by good health and a sound diet? What is the best way to bring up our children? Are we capable of living in harmony with our environment?

Unfortunately, fewer and fewer hunting societies remain. Their numbers have been rapidly reduced since the development of agriculture, by the more numerous and powerful farming peoples. But there is still a little time to help the remaining representatives of natural man choose a meaningful and dignified future for themselves. If we do, we will benefit from the great many things of lasting value they have to teach us. Perhaps in the process we may find a better future for ourselves.

From Apes to Man

Man has become man through the complex process of evolution. Given different environmental pressures at different points in his evolutionary development, he might have become a very different creature. Man belongs to a group of mammals called primates and his nearest relatives are the apes. He and the apes share the same ancestors, an idea some humans have found humiliating. One woman is said to have reacted to Darwin's theory of evolution with the exclamation: "Descended from the apes! My dear, we will hope that it is not true. But if it is, let us pray that it may not become generally known."

Man differs physically from his fellow primates in a number of important respects. He is unable to grasp with his feet. Formerly his big toes may have had the same capacity as his thumbs, as do those of the majority of the other primates. Most of the primates are tropical forest dwellers. They use their hands and feet for grasping branches rather than for walking on the ground. Man's ability to stand upright has enabled him to use his feet for walking and his hands for doing all kinds of intricate work involving great dexterity.

In some other respects, however, man is more or less the same as other primates, retaining features that reflect his forest background. His teeth, as with those of all primates, are multipurpose. They are not specialized as are those of cows for chewing grass, squirrels for gnawing nuts, and tigers for tearing meat. Rather, they are capable of dealing with a variety of foods, vegetable and animal. The position of our eyes is roughly the same as that of other primates. Most of the animals have eyes on either side of their heads, so possessing a wide range of vision. We have them in front, which reduces their horizontal range, but enables us to see an object with both eyes at once. This is a vital attribute for judging distances accurately, of the greatest importance to animals that live in trees.

Our closest relatives are the members of the two ape families—that containing the gibbons, and that containing the chimpanzee, the gorilla, and the orang-utan. We share with them the lack of a tail, the disposition of our internal organs, and much of the structure of the brain.

The oldest remains of an apelike creature dis-

Orangutans (left) share the same ancestors as man. They have become successfully adapted to their forest environment in Southeast Asia. Man, however, has become adapted to a great many environments besides the forests of the tropics. The Australian Aborigine above, for example, was able to survive successively in grassland, scrub, and desert.

Richard Leakey with the skull found by his colleagues near Lake Rudolf in northern Kenya. His preliminary datings suggest it is some 2.9 million years old. The skull is exciting evidence that the genus Homo *may be much older than has been believed.*

covered so far are those of *Parapithecus*, found in the lower Oligocene strata of Egypt and some 30 million years old. Part of it resembles the modern tarsier, a primate but not an ape or a monkey. This lends some support to a much disputed theory that men, apes, and monkeys are descended from tarsierlike ancestors. Many more apelike remains have been found in the Miocene strata (12–26 million years old) of Africa and Asia. Some resemble the modern gibbons, chimpanzees, gorillas, and orang-utans. One, *Proconsul*, looks as if it might have been an ancestor of the chimpanzee, although it has a number of manlike features. The fossil apes, *Dryopithecus*, also have manlike attributes, notably their arms and legs, which look as if they were less specialized for tree-dwelling than those of the modern apes.

The most controversial of the manlike apes is *Australopithecus*. A number of its remains have been found in Africa, but opinion is divided as to whether it is an ancestor of man. The recent discovery by Richard Leakey of a skull as old as *Australopithecus* is certainly an oddity. Some skulls have been found in caves with the remains of the crushed bones of other animals as well as cracked shells. This has led to *Australopithecus* being described as "an animal-hunting, flesh-eating, shell-cracking, and bone-breaking ape."

But no modern ape has a diet like this.

Part of our difficulty in tracing the evolutionary story of the apes and man is due to the environment in which they lived. We know that mankind was born in the forests of the tropics and developed in the grasslands. But tropical forests are probably the least favorable places for the preservation of fossil remains. Thus, it is extremely difficult to discover how man left the forests, in what form, and exactly how he has changed since then. Archaeologists and prehistorians are not yet in a position to answer precisely the question: "Where did modern man come from?"

One thing we can be sure of. Modern man did not come from one single spot in the world. This is not how evolution works. We are the result of a considerable intermingling of races of different evolutionary stages of man over a very wide area. For example, toward the end of the Pleistocene ice age, Europe, western Asia, and North Africa were inhabited by the Neanderthal race, *Homo sapiens neanderthalensis*. These people were no more than five feet tall, but were heavily built, with thick necks, large heads, and in some cases bigger brains than ours. Their bones were heavy, their jaws massive with big teeth, and they stooped. About 75,000 years ago, the Neander-

The diagram (right) shows the changes in proportion between the brain (colored area) and face as man evolved. Compared with chimpanzees, modern man has a much larger brain, about twice the size of that of the great apes. This increase in brain size is associated with the development of speech, improved memory and ability to store information, and especially, the ability to reason.

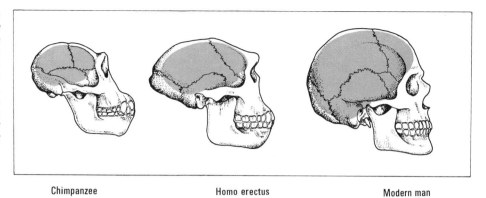

Chimpanzee   Homo erectus   Modern man

Above: the skull found by the Leakey team. In shape it is more like that of modern man than that of Australopithecus, but the cranial capacity is rather small.

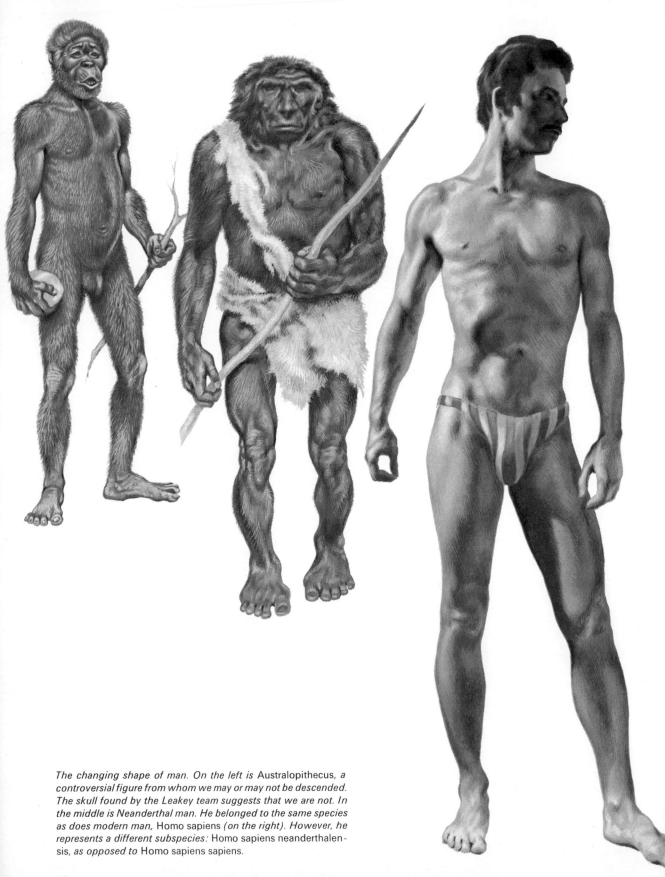

The changing shape of man. On the left is Australopithecus, a controversial figure from whom we may or may not be descended. The skull found by the Leakey team suggests that we are not. In the middle is Neanderthal man. He belonged to the same species as does modern man, Homo sapiens (on the right). However, he represents a different subspecies: Homo sapiens neanderthalensis, as opposed to Homo sapiens sapiens.

thals were replaced by a race that is very definitely modern man, representatives of *Homo sapiens sapiens*. These people also had large brains, were up to six feet tall, and are called Cro-Magnons.

It is not known precisely where the Cro-Magnons came from, although a clue has been found in the series of human bones found in the caves of Mount Carmel, Israel. These range from Neanderthal-type bones to Cro-Magnon-type ones. It is therefore possible that the ancestors of the Cro-Magnons moved north from Africa and that Israel was where the two races met. Probably the Cro-Magnons interbred with the Neanderthals, but the former eventually replaced the latter by virtue of their superior disease resistance and culture inventiveness. Some anthropologists have suggested that there are modern European populations which still carry a few Neanderthal genes.

Why did man leave the trees and lose his particularly apelike characteristics? We can only speculate. Possibly his ancestors lived at the margins of the forest. Maybe this was because, by an accident of genetics, they were not as skilled as the other primates at moving about the trees. More probably, they were simply better adapted to the forest edges. By modifying their diet and behavior they could utilize clearings and the productive forest edges. Individuals would obviously have encountered each other and bred together. Naturally, these individuals would have had more chance of survival and would have been genetically favored. Gradually, distinct populations would have emerged, able to utilize a greater variety of environments, such as grasslands, than conventional apes. These populations would have developed those characteristics likely to improve their utilization of such environments: the ability to walk, to handle a greater diversity of objects, to eat a greater range of foodstuffs. Above all, as apes evolved into men, they ceased to specialize.

Man is not the fastest running animal, nor the strongest swimmer. He is not the strongest animal, nor the most agile climber. He is not unique as a tool-user. He is not the only creature that can dwell in grasslands, forests, mountains, or even deserts. But no other animal is capable of doing all of these things, as man is.

Among those features unique to man are his ability to tolerate a greater range of environments than other species and also his ability to conceptualize, for which he had to develop his brain. Each enlargement of his brain improved his capacity to conceptualize and each improvement in his capacity to conceptualize improved his survival—which in turn favored those human beings with the more developed brains.

Thus by degrees there emerged a new species. Exactly when it did so is very difficult to say. It depends entirely on one's definition of man. Is the upright posture most significant? Or his tool-making abilities? Or his cranial capacity? At all events, the latest date is 600,000 years ago; while the earliest date may be pushed back by Leakey's skull discovery to roughly 3 million years ago.

Evolution ends only with extinction. We may take it that, like all species, we are still subject to the evolutionary process. But for some time now, the pace of man-induced change has been so fast—and is getting faster—that we have not responded with conventional biological adaptations. Rather, we are adjusting culturally, evolving new institutions and behavior patterns. We are not unique in this. There is the famous example of the English blue tits, which have learned to peck through the tops of bottles of milk, so that they can get at the cream. They did not have to develop new beak structures to do this. They simply developed a new behavior pattern, a new habit.

This cultural adaptation has one obvious advantage over physiological adaptation: it is much faster. However, it has one great disadvantage, too. It permits a species the illusion of full adaptation. For example, as a species we have evolved under sugar-scarce conditions. The sugar in our diet used to come only from what was naturally present in ordinary plants and from honey. It is to be expected, therefore, that as soon as we started eating sugar in large quantities, our bodies would show signs of maladaptation. So, of course, we have bad teeth. As a result, we have introduced the cultural adaptation of the dentist, who in effect enables us to go on having bad teeth.

A study of human evolution teaches us about the remarkable flexibility and adaptability of man. But it also teaches us that evolution proceeds fairly slowly, and that we might be wise not to attempt to impose too many sharp changes on ourselves too quickly. The nature of our more inflexible biological and psychological requirements can be appreciated best from a study of our past and in particular from that most fascinating part of it, the era of natural man.

One of man's most remarkable qualities is his ability to live in environments as different as the tropical rain forests and the Arctic coast. On the left are Pygmy hunters of the tropical rain forests of Zaire. On the right is an Eskimo hunter in his kayak.

!Kung Bushmen of the Kalahari

The Bushmen of southern Africa are the most thoroughly studied surviving examples of natural man. Before they came under pressure from alien white and black peoples they inhabited the whole of the region, but now those that remain as hunter-gatherers are largely confined to the least hospitable areas of Botswana, with scattered outliers in Zambia, Rhodesia, Angola, the Namib Desert, and the Transvaal of South Africa. Most of the 55,000 Bushmen alive today have become laborers and stockmen on farms and ranches, or vagrants on the fringes of them; but there are still some 1600 Bushmen in Botswana, living by hunting game and gathering wild plants, more or less as their ancestors have done for many thousands of years.

The land is poor, with very little rain. There are no permanent rivers, although after exceptionally heavy rain low-lying areas become flooded. These flooded areas eventually shrink to pools that can hold water for up to six months after the end of the rainy season.

Although it is so poorly watered this part of the Kalahari Desert is not really desert at all. It is relatively thick thorn scrub, with many trees such as acacias, interspersed with other broad-leaved trees and shrubs. Nonetheless, the environment is harsh enough to make it extremely difficult, if not impossible, for the uninitiated to survive in it—and it is certainly less fertile than the country that supported the majority of Bushmen in their heyday.

Yet they live well. The Dobe !Kung (the exclamation mark denotes a click sound made by the tongue on the roof of the mouth), who are the best known of the Bushmen, eat more protein than the British. Indeed, each person's daily protein intake, 93.1 grams, is exceeded by only 10 countries today. A third of their protein comes from meat, principally warthog, kudu, duiker, and steenbok, followed by gemsbok, wildebeest, springhaas, and guinea fowl. The rest comes from a remarkable nut, the mongongo or mangetti nut, which also has a very high content of other important nutrients and calories. It gives a large crop, can withstand prolonged periods of drought, and can lie on the ground for as long as a year without rotting.

The lush environment of southern Cape Province, South Africa. Before the arrival from the north of Bantu tribes, the native Bushmen enjoyed these surroundings unchallenged.

A herd of wildebeest in the Kalahari Park. These animals are an important source of meat for the Bushmen. On the right a Bushman hunter displays his weapons and a typical array of plant foods. Both these pictures show how arid are the desert and scrubland in which the Bushmen live, in contrast to the richer areas formerly available to them, yet they still eat well.

A Bushman hut. It is made by the women from grass and sticks, and is easily assembled. It provides adequate shelter from sun, rain, or wind, although when the nights grow cold, as they often do, people sleep outside around the fire.

The food supply is varied and remarkably easy to obtain. A time-and-motion study has been made of the hours spent by adult Bushmen hunting and gathering. It was found that they never spent more than 32 hours a week searching for food, and that the average was half that—or just over two hours a day for a seven-day week!

Bushmen communities consist of camps, which vary in size throughout the year. Each camp is based on a waterhole, is largest during the rains, and breaks up into units as small as a single family during periods of drought. At such times, the only sources of moisture might be the fluids from a newly killed animal and melon juice.

Camps constantly fluctuate in size irrespective of the availability of water. This is because the communities have no rigid social structure, but are simply groupings of relations and friends, who get on well together, and find it convenient and pleasant to work and live with each other.

Right: each Bushman camp is based on a water hole. Here a woman on a foraging expedition drinks at a desert pool.

Men do the hunting. Women gather the plants. The men will hunt either alone or in pairs, and will normally cover between 8 and 15 miles in search of an animal. Sometimes a hunter is unlucky and finds nothing, in which case he will probably return with nuts, roots, and perhaps an animal such as the leopard tortoise, which is easily caught, so that he won't arrive in camp empty-handed. It is most unusual for a hunter to bother to stay out all night. He knows that some-

Above left: !Kung Bushman hunters returning to camp with a duiker, a small antelope. Above right: Bushman arrow poison is made from grubs (top) by crushing them in a bowl (lower) made from the kneecap of a giraffe.

thing is bound to turn up another day.

When the hunter comes across the track of an animal, he trails it until he is almost upon it. This requires stealth and a good knowledge of animal behavior. He must get close because his bow is small and weak, and will shoot accurately only over short distances, What kills the animal is the poison applied to the arrow-tips. The poison, taken from grubs, is potent but non-persistent. This means that the animal dies over-night, but by the time the meat is butchered it is perfectly safe to eat.

Once he has shot his prey, the !Kung hunter does not bother to follow it. He knows that if he does so, the animal will only run farther away. If he has shot it early in the morning, he will seek out some of the other men, and together they will butcher it into pieces small enough to carry back to the camp. If the animal is killed in the after-noon, it will not be butchered until the following morning. There is then the possiblity that the body will be plundered by a lion or hyena, but this is a risk that the Bushmen accept.

In groups of three to five the women gather plants. Besides mongongo nuts, they collect baobab fruit, sour plums, marula nuts, melons, and various roots. These are carried home in the women's karosses, garments that serve as dress and carrying bag. The women are generally back by mid-afternoon and never stay out overnight.

A man hunts and a woman gathers whenever he or she want to. Nobody tells them to do any-thing. On any given day, no more than a half, and on average a third, of the able-bodied adults will be out getting food. The rest will be relaxing, making and repairing tools, fashioning ostrich

Three Bushmen catching a springhaas (or Cape jumping hare, a large rodent). Above, one of them has dug a hole, then another prods the animal out if its burrow with a long pole. Below, the digger grabs the animal as it rushes from the scooped-out hole.

Bushman women with the melons they have collected. These are a useful source of water as well as food.

A !Kung Bushman scraping a skin in front of his hut. Animal hides are never wasted. They are used to make karosses, combined cloaks and carrying bags for use by the women, and smaller skins are made into slings for carrying infants.

eggshell jewelry, gossiping, entertaining visitors, or themselves visiting relatives and friends. The men spend much of their time discussing hunting, the whereabouts of game, and so on. They work slightly longer hours than the women, but less regularly. The women will probably work all morning and for much of the afternoon for two to three days a week: plants are reliable and stay put, so their collection can be made a fairly routine activity. By contrast, because the movements of game are so irregular, a man might work intensively for three to four days and then do nothing for weeks. He may have bad luck, be off form, or feel it inappropriate for him to hunt.

With the !Kung people, this seemingly casual and unconcerned activity yields an abundance of vegetable foods, and for each man, woman, and child, on average a half pound of good meat every day. There are three reasons why this is so. First, although the Kalahari scrub might seem inhospitable to us, familiar as we are with lush meadows and well-stocked supermarkets, it is in fact quite rich in food resources. Secondly, the Bushmen have considerable expertise on the whereabouts and properties of plants and on the behavior of animals, which they utilize with

great skill. And thirdly, the Bushmen share whatever they have.

The Bushman ethic of sharing is most important. It means that nobody, young or old, goes in want. Plants are shared only among the women's immediate family, including aged dependants. All able-bodied women gather, and their two to three days' work is enough for a week's supply. If, however, a woman has been unable to collect anything, she will be supplied by her companions.

Meat, on the other hand, is shared throughout the camp. Strictly speaking it belongs to the owner of the first arrow to lodge in the animal, and this may not necessarily be the hunter, and could be a woman. The meat is first divided between the arrow-owner and the members of the party who helped to hunt and butcher it. Each then distributes his share, a man giving first to his wife's parents, then to his own, then to his wife and children, followed by his brothers and sisters and those of his wife, and finally to any of his other relations who are there, to his friends, and those from whom he has received meat in the past. Each of the people to whom he has given meat will in turn give some of his share to others, adopting a similar order of priorities.

This regular pattern of exchange ensures that everybody in camp is given meat and that over a period of time everybody's share is equal.

Because they are confident of their environment's constant ability to yield food, the !Kung make no attempt to create a surplus. They store nothing, and would consider anybody who did so an antisocial hoarder.

Sharing is not confined to meat. Nothing that is not essential for survival, such as a bow or a kaross, is regarded as a personal possession. Jewelry or any other nonessential item might be "owned" by an individual, but someone else need only ask to borrow it, and he will not be refused. Such "possessions" often go through a long process of borrowing and sharing, a practice that reinforces individual relationships. Indeed, the whole custom of sharing is very important for social cohesion.

The main practical reason why the Bushmen are not acquisitive is that they are nomadic. Nobody wants to be burdened with possessions when he or she moves around a lot and has to carry them. Since the Bushmen have no pack animals, the total weight of each individual's possessions never exceeds 25 pounds, a load that is easily borne. A family's belongings, for example bow and arrows, musical instruments, pipes, cooking pots, water pots, jewelry, and children's toys, will go into a pair of sacks no larger than overnight bags.

This lack of acquisitiveness, besides being sensible, has been elevated into a social value. Generosity, nonviolence, and a propensity for laughter, are considered admirable virtues.

The sharing ethic also means that old people are looked after, long after they have ceased to be "productive," even in the unusual event that the old person is without relatives. The proportion of men and women over 60 is 10 per cent—smaller than in the industrial countries of Europe and North America, but significantly greater than in the nonindustrial countries of the tropics. Similarly, the level of infant mortality lies between that of the rich third of the world and the higher rate of the poor two-thirds.

Generally speaking, the life of the !Kung Bushmen is not only easy, but also relatively free from disease. Their happy physical circumstances are matched by a harmonious social life, of which the sharing ethic is but one example. This is not to say that life is entirely free of tensions. But the !Kung fear violence and try to avoid conflict.

Above: !Kung Bushmen sharing meat. Meat from all but the smallest animals is always shared out according to a set pattern. These are Nyae Nyae !Kung, and they are not so well-off as the Dobe !Kung, described in the text.

Left: a group of Bushman children and old and middle-aged women talking. The anthropologist Richard Lee reports that 10 per cent of the population of the groups he studied were over 60 years old, and some were considerably older.

!Kung parents often try to arrange marriages, but their attempts are rarely more successful than any modern parent's attempts at match-making. Trial marriages are common, and between the ages of puberty and the age of 30 an individual may go through a number of experimental marriages. During this period, too, divorces are common; the person who wants the divorce simply leaves the other. Friendly relations are generally quickly restored, and sometimes an estranged couple will live with their new partners in the same camp.

Once they are past the age of 30, however,

An old Bushman in a medicine (trance) dance. The dance is an important way of maintaining harmony in the community, and occurs spontaneously about once a week in a large camp.

tive people in the world." It is very difficult for an outsider to distinguish between a dialogue of exaggerated abuse and a real dispute. Most arguments rage and then collapse in verbal battles of Shakespearean richness. In the middle of the uproar a bystander might crack a joke or one of the antagonists might make a particularly absurd play on words: the whole camp dissolves in laughter, and the dispute is over.

Occasionally, however, the grievance is more serious, in which case other members of the camp have to intervene to keep the peace. If this happens, a few days will elapse and then one or both of the disputants will leave with their immediate family. The dispute will not be given as the reason for their departure, but some pretext will be chosen such as the intention of going off to a different area where the food-plants are said to be better or the game more abundant.

Camp fission—the practice of leaving one camp for another, so that each camp is in a constant state of flux—is a most effective way of avoiding violence. Yet sometimes, as in all communities, tensions are more general and widespread, and something less ordinary, more dramatic, is required to resolve them. This is the trance dance.

The trance dance is also called the medicine dance, for its explicit function is not simply to release tensions, but to cure sick individuals. More accurately, the acknowledged motive for such dances will be either entertainment—the expression of sheer *joie de vivre* as when the hunting has gone particularly well or when there are a lot of welcome visitors in camp—or healing. In any case, some curing will be done by the men in trance; and whatever the stated motive, the dance's most valuable function remains the relief of tension.

Trance dances occur on average once a week in large camps, once a month in small ones, although being spontaneous their frequency varies greatly. The women sit in a circle, shoulder to shoulder, facing the fire. They provide the music by singing and clapping. The songs and rhythms are traditional, but the women enjoy inventing variations on them. The men dance around them, moving counter-clockwise and clockwise by turns. The old people and the children sit around separate fires outside the dance circle.

The dance does not begin until after dark. Some of the women light a fire and begin to sing. They are joined by others, and the men are stimulated to dance. Only their legs move, the

Bushmen stabilize their marital life and their marriages become permanent. The constancy and resilience of the relationship thereafter is possibly due to the great deal of liberty both parties enjoyed beforehand.

Often the man will have undergone some sort of probationary period with his wife's parents, who wanted to assure themselves of his qualities, particularly his ability to bring back meat. The length of this period varies, of course, and is subject to the inevitable fluctuations of camp life.

!Kung Bushmen enjoy a good argument. They have been described as "among the most talka-

This old man is in a trance and is laying his hands on another man, thus "curing" him.

rest of their bodies remaining quite stiff. Their feet stamp out a vigorous, highly syncopated beat. After about two hours, the men start to go into a trance. No drugs are used: the trance is due entirely to the high degree of concentration, to a decrease of carbon dioxide in the blood caused by the dancer's rapid and deep breathing, and to auto-suggestion. Those who first go into trance are supported by their companions who are still awake. Once they are fully in trance, the men move among the singers and spectators, especially those who are sick, "curing" them by laying their hands on them. This is the high point of the dance. Naturally the men do not go into trance simultaneously, but after each one has done so, and has performed the act of curing, he will go into a very deep sleep. The dance usually lasts all night—its most intense periods being just after midnight and at dawn—so it is very exhausting.

It is not easy to bear the intense experience of

Above: a Mbuti Pygmy camp in a clearing in the rain forests of Zaire, with its intimate association of human dwelling and natural habitat. In many places all over the world people have exchanged similar such environments for other, less congenial habitats such as this Hong Kong shanty town (right).

the trance dance, and young men often go charging into the bush or into the fire at the center of the circle of singing women. Since they might knock themselves out or seriously burn themselves or someone else, the more experienced men have to restrain them. When he is experienced, a man can channel his emotional energy and go into controlled trance, often twice a night.

Obviously a 12-hour trance of this nature has a purging effect on the community, involving as it does everybody in camp. In the course of this extremely intense experience any residual tensions still left, despite the various ways employed by the Bushmen to reduce them, are released.

According to Thomas Hobbes, the 17th-century political philosopher, life in the state of nature was "solitary, poor, nasty, brutish, and short." He had no evidence for this assertion—indeed there is a good deal of evidence to the contrary.

We have seen that, despite their comparatively unfavorable environment, the Bushmen of the Kalahari enjoy a life of reasonable abundance, longevity, good health, harmony, and entertainment. Although Europeans and Americans might find it uncomfortable, they should bear in mind that the Bushman standard of living is exceeded by only a minority of those people alive today.

We know that, before they were pushed out by more powerful farmers and herdsmen, most of the Bushmen lived in much more generous environments than that of the Kalahari, and we may safely assume that their standard of living was consequently even higher.

The best accounts of those other surviving hunter-gathers whose homes are in the most favorable parts of the tropics (between latitudes 30° North and South) show (although not so precisely) that their lives until recently were also good. In fact, it is probable that all hunter-gatherers living in environments to which they were adapted enjoyed high-quality lives.

This is especially significant when we consider that all but a minority of mankind have been hunter-gatherers living in just such environments. The skull found at East Rudolf in Kenya by Richard Leakey is evidence that men have been around for almost 3 million years. For 99 per cent of this time they lived by hunting and gathering, much as the Bushmen do today. Of the estimated 80,000 million men who have ever lived, only six per cent have done so by agriculture, less than four per cent by industry, and the rest by hunting and gathering.

It is therefore probable that abject poverty, squalor, epidemic diseases, and senseless violence are, in fact, recent aberrations. We have come to regard them as our natural lot, unless we can be protected from them by our technological ingenuity and the legislatures and bureaucracies of our industrial civilization. Mankind was spared them for the greater part of his experience. However, that is not to claim that conflict, illness, and hardship were absent, simply no more prevalent than among the other higher animals.

What went wrong? If it is true that for thous-

The Lewis Glacier, Mount Kenya. Extreme climatic and environmental changes caused at the end of the Pleistocene glaciation may well have disrupted man's stable relationship with the rest of nature, provoking his still continuing population explosion.

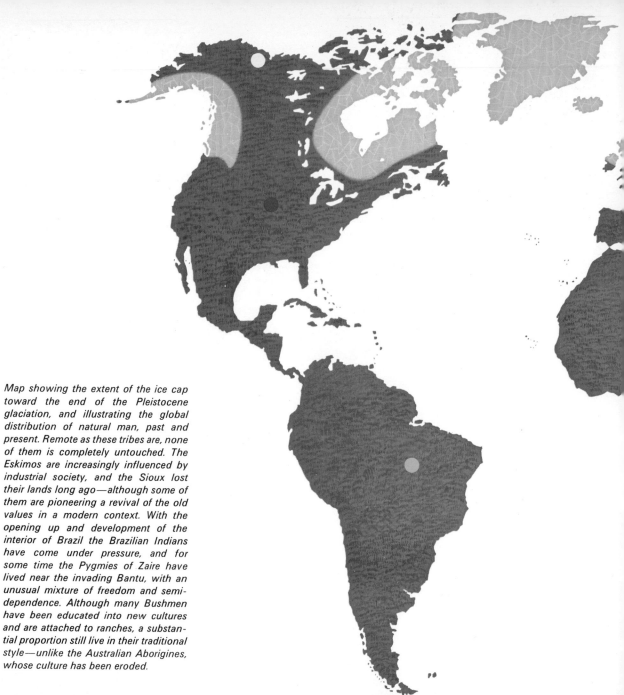

Map showing the extent of the ice cap toward the end of the Pleistocene glaciation, and illustrating the global distribution of natural man, past and present. Remote as these tribes are, none of them is completely untouched. The Eskimos are increasingly influenced by industrial society, and the Sioux lost their lands long ago—although some of them are pioneering a revival of the old values in a modern context. With the opening up and development of the interior of Brazil the Brazilian Indians have come under pressure, and for some time the Pygmies of Zaire have lived near the invading Bantu, with an unusual mixture of freedom and semi-dependence. Although many Bushmen have been educated into new cultures and are attached to ranches, a substantial proportion still live in their traditional style—unlike the Australian Aborigines, whose culture has been eroded.

Eskimos   Sioux Indians   Brazilian Indians *Beiços de Pan*

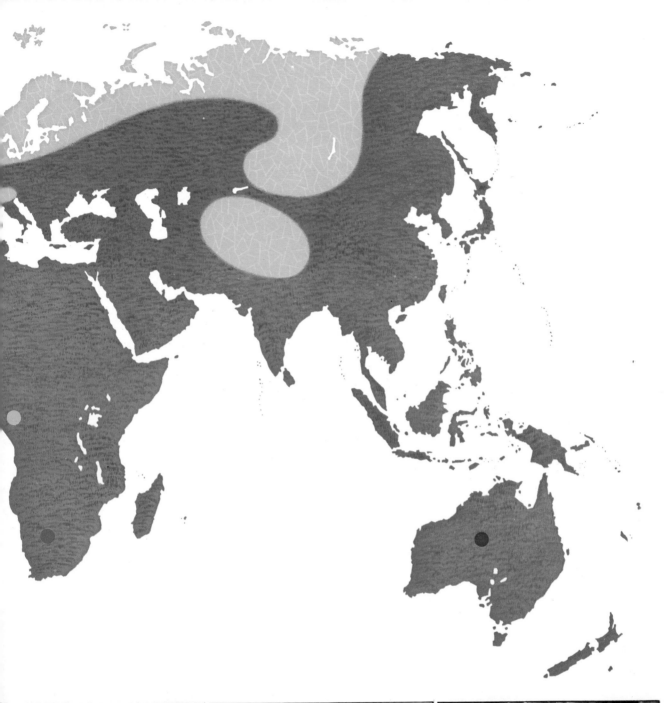

Pygmies

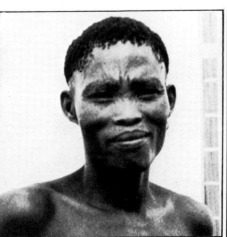

● Bushmen

● Aborigines

ands of years men enjoyed a high standard of living—so high that it was not bettered for a significant proportion of the Western population until after the Industrial Revolution—why did he throw it all away? Why didn't he know what was good for him?

We can only guess. We know that until about 11,000 years ago, the human population was small and stable. In the past people believed that this was due to a suppression by crude environmental factors such as disease and famine, much as it was in our more recent past before the development of public sanitation and so on. Now careful, less prejudiced studies of anthropologists over the last 30 years have revealed enough evidence to strongly suggest that the role of crude environmental factors was insignificant. Our ancestors' populations must have been regulated in part by infant mortality, but largely by infanticide, abortion, and contraception.

Obviously individual couples must have had strong pressures upon them to make them resort to these methods. That of hardship would be easy to understand, but, with conditions as favorable as they were, plainly hardship did not apply. It is most likely that there were certain cultural controls, impulses built into the culture, which stimulated communities into regulating their numbers before they exceeded the carrying capacity of the environment. We have very little idea what these cultural controls were, but we know they must have been related in some way to environmental conditions. Many other animals regulate their populations, and it has been found that the secret of their success is a subtle early warning from the habitat—such as an artificial, socially determined notion of density—which triggers off population control. This is plainly more adaptive (and more pleasant) that breeding right up to the point of collapse from starvation or epidemic, or both.

So it must have been with men. A part of the complex relationship between culture and environment was a feedback that triggered off the

As man's population grew too large to be sustained by the hunting way of life, he was forced to turn to agriculture and the domestication of animals. Relatively early on, he developed the remarkably efficient system of the rice paddy. This photograph shows rice terraces in the Philippines.

mechanisms of population regulation before the habitat was jeopardized.

These controls were of course unconscious. They had to be, otherwise anybody could modify or abandon them for, no doubt, excellent short term reasons, but with disastrous consequences in the long term. However, there is one inevitable disadvantage to internal controls of this nature; they are incapable of responding to conditions outside their evolutionary experience. All organisms are capable of adaptation, man no less than the others, but it is a basic law of all biological systems that there is an optimum level of adaptation. If an organism adapted to every conceivable change in the environment, it would be incapable of adapting to normal conditions of stability. Thus organisms such as man tend to be able to adapt only to a given range of change; if the change is too radical the species will be unable to adapt to it.

The last great advance and retreat of the Pleistocene ice cap between 12,000 and 9000 years ago, caused tremendous changes in climate. These, in turn, caused marked modifications of the environment, so marked that entire species of game were wiped out or were forced to move to other areas. They were followed by man, who now found himself in environments of which he had inadequate evolutionary experience. The controls that formerly regulated both his numbers and his relationships with other species could no longer operate. This enormously accelerated the dispersals and movements of mankind, which brought about the extinction of many Pleistocene animal species, the population by man of the Americas, and the domestication of plants and animals.

Some peoples remained in the environments they knew and maintained stability. A few others restabilized at a later date. They were quickly outnumbered, for the majority embarked on an expansionist course that has continued up to the present day: a sharp rise in population until it is suppressed by natural disaster; then comes some technological innovation that counteracts the disaster, and the population expands again. Thus it continued until the introduction of preventive medicine and public sanitation. These two factors released populations from the epidemic diseases brought about by overcrowding, which itself originated at about the same time as farming and stock raising, at the end of the era of natural man.

Left: in sharp contrast with the intensive use of the hillside in the picture opposite, is the ranching of sheep and cattle. Here sheep are being sold in New South Wales, Australia.
Below: a rock painting from the Tassili region of Algeria. It shows that cattle once grazed an area that is now the Sahara Desert.

Natural Man and his Environment

There are five different ways of getting food: hunting, fishing, gathering, agriculture, and the domestication of animals. As we have seen, the first three are natural, farming and stock-raising being recent innovations. It is also believed that man did not start fishing until some time after the beginnings of hunting.

Hunting is the subsistence activity associated most with natural man, although most hunter-gatherers depend on it for no more than 30 to 40 per cent of their total diet (by weight), the rest comes from the gathering of plants. Nevertheless hunting remains as important nutritionally as gathering, and more important psychologically.

This is not surprising. In the first place the eating of meat usually induces a feeling of great well-being. Most people still like nothing better than sitting down to a good steak; and it is really quite amazing how fish is scorned as a substitute for meat, even in those areas where fish are cheaper and easier to obtain. In the second place there is great drama in the hunt, in the idea of man pitting his strength and his wits against another animal—risking himself for a meal for the entire community.

This idea has survived among peoples who are no longer hunter-gatherers. The Majangir of southwest Ethiopia, for example, get most of their food from gardening and honey-collecting, and not more than 15 per cent from hunting. African buffaloes and elephants are the only animals considered to have power or life-force, and of the two the buffalo is preferred for its flesh and the courage and skill required to kill it. Songs and dances about the food quest are mostly concerned with the successful hunting of buffalo.

A number of people consider game the only proper food, whether or not vegetables and fruit make up a greater proportion of their diet. The Bushmen will describe themselves as "hungry" if they have not eaten meat, even though they may have gorged themselves on plant matter.

To this day, hunting plays a part, however minor, in the lives of Europeans and Americans, particularly in the country. Fox hunting, water-fowling, and potshots at pigeons and rabbits testify to the prevailing attachment to the hunt.

Above: a Pygmy hunting a buffalo. This is an unusual picture, as the Pygmies have a healthy respect for buffalo and usually regard hunting them as foolishly risky. Right: two Bushman hunters crouch low as they stalk an animal in open grassland.

There are many hunting techniques—some involving entire bands, others the individual alone. The one requiring most people is the drive, a method suited to open areas such as grassland and tundra, where there are large migratory herds, and where there is relatively little cover for the lone stalker. The Eskimos used to take advantage of the annual migration of the caribou (a kind of reindeer) to drive a herd into a lake. They then took to their boats and shot the animals at leisure. Their kill was never wasted, however, for the meat was stored in ice and the

An Amerindian of the Guiana Highlands rain forest, Venezuela, hunts by stalking with a blowpipe and poisoned darts.

hides cleaned and cured and used for clothing.

The most famous practitioners of the drive were the Indians of the North American plains, who drove buffalo over cliffs or anywhere they could not escape. They were able thus to take herd after herd, and it was not until after the Spaniards had introduced the horse in the 16th century that they gradually developed the art of shooting large numbers of moving individuals.

The drive was also the method used by the Shoshone Indians to take much smaller animals. Men, women, and children drove rabbits down small canyons toward a net, where they were killed with clubs. The Shoshone also hunted even smaller creatures—grasshoppers, cooked ready for the table at the same time as they were caught, by firing the grass.

Many peoples, however, hunt animals individually. This demands patient stalking, and often the hunter disguises himself as one of his prey, wearing its skin, mimicking its call, and sometimes even its movements. Some forms of individual hunting demand great bravery as well as skill; for example, the method of killing elephants practiced by the Mbuti Pygmies of Zaire. One man goes behind the elephant and then dashes in and hamstrings one of the back legs. Another man attacks the other back leg, and when the animal is helpless, the hunters kill it.

Just as much courage was needed by the Eskimo whalers, who in tiny open boats fought the giants of the cold Arctic seas. A handful of men had to control their craft in very difficult waters, while the harpoonist needed excellent balance and judgment to enable him to take the whale without mishap.

The spear, harpoon, and bow and arrow are not the only hunting implements. Quite as important is the trap. The Majangir, for example, take particular advantage of the thick forests in which they live, where animals follow distinct runs. The Majangir place their traps across the runs so that the animals (bush pig, bush buck, duiker, and porcupine) are forced to pass through a noose attached to a large stake. This is bent forward, so that when the noose is released it springs sharply back, killing the animal.

Fishing is the hunting technique of the water, and fish are still hunted on a large scale today. A negligible proportion of the world fish catch is farmed, and however sophisticated are the fishing fleets of the industrial powers the fact

Napore tribesmen gather at the start of a hunt in the Karamoja district of Uganda. These men do not live by hunting, as they are pastoralists (herdsmen), but wild meat is an important supplement to their diet.

remains that the men aboard are hunting. Fishing is also one of the world's most popular sports.

As with land hunting, there are a great many methods and tools for hunting. Some Amerindian peoples are adept at shooting fish with bow and arrow, others at spearing them. But perhaps trapping and poisoning are the most effective.

A remarkable variety of traps are made, ranging from a few bundles of reeds to complex structures made with great care and skill. People such as the Sanpoil, who lived in the plateau area of southwest Canada, took great care of their traps, because they depended upon them for their survival through the hard winters. A Salmon Chief was appointed for the entire period of the salmon runs (from May to October) and his job was to decide who should empty each trap and how the catch should be shared. He had total control over all activities associated with fishing, taking particular care that all the traps were in good order. This included making sure that no woman went too near them, or near any part of the salmon stream for that matter, lest she damage them by her presence alone. If a woman did get too close, the Salmon Chief had to beg the salmon to ignore the offense.

Many of the Indian peoples of South America have a considerable knowledge of fish poisons. The most common method is first to partially dam a stream with branches to minimize the risk of fish escaping. Then to cut down vines and beat them so that the sap runs into the water. The sap has the effect of stupefying the fish, which float to the surface where they can be caught with ease. The poison does not remain in the fish, or at least not in a form that is harmful to humans. There are many such fish poisons, and the Amerindians have an extensive knowledge of them. This knowledge has already helped in the advance of pesticide chemistry (for example, the insecticide Derris is derived from an Amerindian fish poison), and undoubtedly could be utilized much more—in the development of new drugs, for instance.

Once a fish has been caught, of course, it must be kept fresh. It would be extremely difficult in the tropics, for instance, but, since fish is just one of a number of foods eaten there, and its occurrence is regular it is not a problem. However, in areas like the Pacific Coast of Canada fish made

Turkana fishermen with hand nets on Lake Rudolf, Kenya. Netting fish is one more method of hunting invented by man.

A Kalapolo Indian fishing on the Xingu River, Brazil. Great accuracy is displayed in hitting the fish.

up at least half the total food supply and although astonishingly abundant at times they were also scarce at others. Peoples like the Tlingit, the Bella Coola, and the Nootka, had therefore to devise means of storing the fish for months on end, particularly during the snowbound winters.

In the summer, the Bella Coola took immense catches of humpback and sockeye salmon, halibut, and lingcod, and dried them on racks in the sun. In the autumn, other varieties of salmon were taken, such as cohoe and dog, and these were smoked indoors out of the rain. The sockeye and dog salmon kept best because they are fatter than the others.

The fat from the richer fish was often rendered into oil. When the dried fish were eventually eaten they were dipped into this oil, which provided the Indians with valuable fats and carbohydrates. Salmon eggs were allowed to get high and were then made into something resembling cheese. Clams were also preserved, first by steaming and then by drying them. Among some of the peoples of the Pacific coast, the dried fish were kept in pits, but generally they were stored in baskets and boxes that were then placed on racks inside each home. Apparently the smell was quite intense.

On the other side of the Pacific, the Ainu of Japan trained their dogs to catch fish for them. The men used to take 20 or 30 dogs along the shallow sandy bays. At an agreed point, half the men and dogs would stay where they were, while the other half moved on a farther 200 yards or so. At a signal, both groups of dogs would swim out to sea in a single file. Then the men gave a shout and the dogs wheeled around toward each other until the heads of the two files met. Then at another shout the dogs swam ashore in a crescent. Any fish between them and the shore were driven inexorably toward the beach. As soon as it felt the bottom each dog would grab a fish and take it to his master, no one else. His recognized reward was the fish's head. Each man kept the fish brought to him, together with his fair share of any of the fish that had fled onto dry land.

The Ainu were one of a number of food-collecting peoples for whom fish was the most important element in their diet. This is not surprising in view of their geographical position. Most food-collectors living in the far North (North of 60°) depended largely on meat; most of those, like the Ainu and the Bella Coola, who lived in the intermediate latitudes (from 40°–50°) depended largely

A Waura Indian of Brazil, killing a fish by biting it.

on fish; while most of those living in the tropics and subtropics (0°–39°) depended largely on the gathering of plants.

Gathering, like hunting, is still practiced today, more for fun than anything else. People walk the fields and hedgerows in search of nuts, black-berries, and mushrooms, not because it is an essential part of life but because it is a pleasant change from the office, or fun for the kids. Plants

that were once exclusively gathered are either no longer eaten or are deliberately cultivated. The exceptions are seaweed, still gathered in vast quantities by the Japanese and to a lesser extent by the Welsh; truffles, gathered by the French and the Italians simply because they cannot be grown; and, until 1968, wild rice.

Wild rice is, strictly speaking, not a rice at all, but a separate type of grain in its own right. This delicious food, besides being the staple diet of the Chippewa Indians of Minnesota, is highly valued as a luxury by many Americans. Wild rice is still gathered by the Chippewa, even though in most

Ojibwa (Chippewa) Indians still harvest wild rice in the tra-ditional way. Here they assemble on Rice Lake, Minnesota.

other respects they follow an industrial way of life, however impoverished. This is basically because the hand-gathering of the rice is a vital link with the past, but also because it grows in such a way as to make manual harvesting much better for the rice beds than mechanical harvesting. Unfortunately, wild rice is now being grown by white Americans in paddy fields, and thus a valuable and traditional living is progressively being wrested from the Indians.

For most peoples, however, the gathering of wild plants was once of the greatest possible importance. This being the case, it is interesting that it was left almost entirely to the women of each group, while the men were charged with hunting and fishing. Thus, even now, among the Western Desert Aborigines of Australia, women are the chief providers and spend one-third more time than the men on food collection and preparation. Occasionally the men deceive their womenfolk by telling them they are going hunting, and then, once they are well away from the camp, spend the rest of the day on sacred carving or

Ojibwa Indians bagging up the hand-gathered harvest. Strictly speaking the grain is not rice at all, but it is very nutritious.

An Eripagtsa woman from Brazil is watched by her child as she gathers wild honey—a much-sought-after delicacy.

some other activity less strenuous than the hunt. When they return empty-handed, their excuse is one to which the women are fairly well accustomed. They saw little game and the hunting was very difficult, they say.

The Tiwi of northern Australia are well aware of the economic importance of women. In this respect they are considered as more important than men, although this insight is used to justify not women's liberation but polygamy, the marriage of many women to one man. When a missionary once tried to persuade a Tiwi elder with a particularly impressive retinue of wives that this accumulation was impious, the aborigine answered: "If I had only one or two wives I would starve, but with my present 10 or 12 wives I can send them in all directions in the morning and at least two or three of them are likely to bring something back with them at the end of the day, and then we can all eat."

Many sorts of leaves, seeds, roots, fruits, berries, nuts, and mushrooms are gathered, and different groups of food-collectors have differing preferences, from the Mongongo nuts of the Bushmen to the fruit called mundjutj collected by the Aborigines of Arnhem Land. They leave the fruit until it is wrinkled like a prune, then they rub it with a red ocher and allow it to go dry until it is hard and brittle. Wrapped in bark it will keep for months, until it is pounded into a

Some aquatic animals are gathered, not hunted. Here, a group of Australian Aborigines gather shellfish on the shore.

paste, mixed with kangaroo meat, and eaten.

Common to all peoples living in regions warm enough for bees, however, is a passionate fondness for honey. Honey is a food esteemed universally, and especially by natural man. The Majangir method of obtaining it is typical: a few men go off with gourds, an axe or large knife, and fire-sticks. They keep a sharp eye on the trees, and when they see a few bees obviously going in and out of a hole in one of them, they set to work. One man uses the fire-sticks to light a fire, while another takes the axe to the hole to enlarge it. A bundle of twigs chosen for their tendency to smoke is placed on the fire, and when they are smoking they are put by the hole, as it is widened still more. The smoke stupifies the bees, and they allow the men to raid the nest almost unstung.

The combs, dripping with the delicious fluid, are withdrawn and put into the gourds—apart from those that are consumed on the spot. Sometimes a part of the comb is left and the hole repaired, to encourage the bees to return.

During certain months of the year, the Majangir and a number of other peoples are seized with an irresistible craving for honey. The Mbuti Pygmies become obsessed with it, and dance and sing and talk about nothing else. The Majangir take their honey in three ways; straight from the comb, by chewing on the wax until all sweetness is gone, when the wax is spat out; diluted in

The first stage in slash-and-burn gardening. With only a hand-ax, an Amerindian man fells one of the larger trees.

water to make a nonalcoholic and surprisingly refreshing sweet drink; and mixed with water and a special bark that they gather and powder. This mixture is slowly heated overnight, and the fermentation properties of the bark act so fast that by morning a drink has been produced as dry as red wine, with the alcoholic strength of beer, and tasting of honey.

Farming cannot really be said to be a "natural" activity, and different farming methods grade subtly from one to the other. Probably the oldest method is slash-and-burn, or swidden, which consists of first felling the larger trees, then burning off the fallen wood and the scrub, and finally clearing the area ready for sowing.

This method sounds much more destructive than it is: in fact, provided it is practiced by a people whose numbers are stable, it is one of the safest and most productive methods known to man. The closer a group is to the social conditions of the food-collecting way of life, the more stable and natural is their method of cultivation.

Under such conditions, swidden imitates as much as possible the pattern of the surrounding vegetation so that the swidden garden tends to be almost as stable as the environment it has replaced. In the forest regions of the tropics, where slash-and-burn has been most successful, the pattern of vegetation is one of high diversity —a mass of different species. This diversity is duplicated by the swidden cultivators, such as the Tsembaga of New Guinea and the Hanunoo of the Philippines. The latter grow dry rice (that is rice in ordinary gardens, not in paddies), but their rice gardens contain a great many other plants besides. At the sides and against the fences there are often five different kinds of climbing beans. Next to them, toward the center of the garden, there is a mixture of grain crops, root crops, shrubs, and small food-bearing trees. These plants will all be ready for harvesting at the same time of year, when among them the vines of yams and sweet potatoes, and the leaves of the taro betray the presence of a growing store of rootcrops that will be ready some time later. Once the rice toward the center has ripened, it is replaced by the slower growing shrubs and trees.

The combination of so many species of food plants ensures that no time is lost between the ripening of one type of plant and that of another. It also means that the fragile layer of decaying plant and animal matter on the surface is not

The felled trunks and branches are then burned.

A man carrying away timber useful for poles.

destroyed by the direct rays of the sun or washed away by the rain. Instead the nutrients within it are taken up immediately by plants valuable to man. At the same time, of course, the beneficial effects of the sun are utilized to the fullest extent by converting the energy into a productive protective canopy of vegetation. Generally, some of the original trees are retained for the protection they give.

Swidden has been described as a natural forest transformed into a harvestable forest, and it is easy to see why. There is good evidence that slash-and-burn is more productive over the long term than more extensive methods. The Tepoztlan swiddens of Mexico yield double the harvest of continuously cropped fields, and the farmers of the West African hill districts abandoned their swiddens in the valleys for manured terraces only when raiders forced them into the hills.

Slash-and-burn is almost as easy a way of life as hunting and gathering. With only two hours' work a day, the South American Kuikuru can grow an acre of manioc. This provides some four million calories a year—so much that they can allow up to half the crop to be robbed by peccaries and ants.

As with hunting and gathering, so with farming there is division of labor between the sexes. The men do the heavy work of felling the trees, burning the debris, and clearing the ground; the women do the planting and harvesting. A swidden patch will last from three to seven years depend-

ing on its location, and yielding less and less each year as the nutrients are consumed. It must then lie fallow for 5 to 15 years. The forest is allowed to return, which it does in the form of secondary growth—the unkempt mass of vines, shrubs, and trees that people associate with the jungle of adventure stories. If the secondary growth were left alone it would gradually be replaced by true forest, but normally after 15 years at most the nutrient cycle is sufficiently re-established for the growth to be cleared for yet another garden.

Although this means that each man would not have to clear a new garden very often, if he worked by himself he would have infrequent bouts of intensely back-breaking work. But in fact the men co-operate with one another, thus providing longer periods of more continuous—and less strenuous—work.

Different peoples have different staples—the crop on which they depend most. In Southeast Asia it is rice, in the forests of Africa it is yams, and in the African grasslands it is millet and sorghum. At the time Europeans first came to the Americas, the Indians were growing about 120 different plant species, of which maize was the staple in North America and the Central American highlands, potatoes in the Andes, and manioc (cassava) in the forests of Central and South America. It is somewhat startling that modern man has not domesticated any new staples—that all of our major food plants were domesticated

Clearing the garden (left) and harvesting (above). The men do the heavy work of clearing and preparing the gardens; but the women do the planting and sowing, look after the plants, and then finally harvest the produce.

51

shortly after man ceased to be truly natural. All we have done is improve on the work of farmers very much like the people still practicing slash-and-burn today.

Herdsmen are the true nomads of the world, roaming over much greater distances than hunter-gatherers who, although they move around much more than we do, tend to do so in a relatively confined area. Most herdsmen, on the other hand, will stay put only until their animals have grazed out the area and they are forced to move on, covering great distances in this way.

Generally, the animals domesticated by herdsmen, or pastoralists as they are known, were once native to the area—for example, the reindeer of the Lapps in Europe's Arctic north. There is one great exception to this rule, however. The cattle of the African pastoralists—the Fulani of West Africa, the Masai astride the borders of Kenya and Tanzania, and the Karamojong in the wildest part of Uganda—were introduced into Africa from Asia about 4000 years ago, but since then

they have become a dominant part of the African scene. To people like the Masai and the Karamojong they are a source not simply of food, but also of riches and prestige. The main food of these herdsmen is cow's milk and the blood obtained by cutting the jugular vein in the cow's neck. Only a small incision is made, so that the cow can continue giving blood with as little ill effect as we suffer when we donate blood to the hospital blood bank. Cattle are a measure of a man's wealth and a constant source of pride to the Masai. He will part with a cow only with the greatest reluctance, as for example, when he has to pay the bride price.

Domestic animals are important, not merely to pure pastoralists, but to less specialized farmers as well. Among the Melanesian peoples of New Guinea and the smaller islands of the western Pacific, pigs are valued socially as much as they are nutritionally. For example, the Bomagai-Angoiang of New Guinea give every one of their pigs personal names and practically make them part of the family. Pigs are always part of

Above: reindeer are the only species of deer to have been domesticated. Few kinds of animals have been domesticated by man.

the bride price, and are killed whenever someone is ill or dies. They play an important part in the ceremonial life of New Guinean peoples—ceremonies, and occasionally even wars, occurring only when pigs are in good supply, so that a fine feast is assured.

Although generally the pigs are owned by the men, they are looked after by the women, who can cope easily with one or two, but begin to grumble if they have to care for more. The attitude of the men, however, is that the only good pig is a cooked pig and in the tedious period between birth and the pot, pigs must stay with the women. As one anthropologist, writing of a people called the Karam, puts it: they feel that "women are always potentially dangerous because of their child-bearing capacities and menstrual activities, but you have to live with them. Pigs are also filthy creatures, but you have to live with them too."

Masai herdsmen of Kenya and Tanzania with their cattle.

Young Turkana boys tending a herd of camels. Among pastoral peoples children start work early in life.

Now that Eskimos have high-powered rifles, their one-time respect for animals has changed to relative indifference.

From the very moment of birth, hunter-gatherers and hunter-gardeners are made aware of their intimate relationship with the rest of Nature. The Hupa of northern California used to take the remains of the infant's umbilical cord and place it in a young spruce. They believed that the child would be identified with the tree and grow as strongly. The Polynesian Tokelau follow a similar custom, placing the afterbirth and umbilical cord in the ground, and planting over it a coconut tree, thereafter regarded as the child's.

Many North American Indian tribes sent their adolescent boys on spirit quests. They would go alone into the forests and mountains, fending entirely for themselves, until they were visited by the spirit of a plant or animal. This would then be their guardian for the rest of their lives, and would aid them in the hunt.

Natural man does not distinguish quite as sharply as we do between man and the other animals or between man and the rest of Nature. He has a much more realistic appreciation of the interdependency of man and the living world about him. This awareness is expressed in ways that we might find sentimental or mystical or just odd, although an increasing number of people today are coming to realize that natural man's religious attitude to his fellow species is probably more scientific than our mixture of indifference and hostility. Certainly it is more conducive to survival in the long term.

The Eskimos had every reason to feel hostility

Above right: an Eskimo hunter alone in the harsh environment he has learned to come to terms with. Below: an Eskimo woman cooking seal meat. None of the animal is wasted.

toward their incredibly harsh environment, yet they did not. In the business of kill or starve, which so many people, ignorant of the abattoir and the factory farm, now find so cruelly uncivilized, the Eskimo was well aware that he had no more right to live and eat than did his prey. Consequently, he developed a strictly moral code of behavior toward the animals he hunted. Whenever a polar bear, or a seal, or a whale (any mammal in fact that came from the sea) was killed, the wife of the hunter would welcome the spirit of the dead creature, offer it a cup of fresh water, and ask it to return to its fellows to tell them that it had been treated properly.

The Nemadi of Mauretania hunt the addax, an antelope of the Sahara Desert. Whenever a Nemadi hunter is about to kill one he asks its forgiveness. Sometimes the respect given to animals by hunting peoples is extended even to highly dangerous ones. For example, the G/wi (the stroke denotes a click sound made by the teeth) Bushmen of Botswana have been seen to remove scorpions carefully from the camp to prevent them straying into the fire. And the Dorobo of Kenya will not kill any snake that enters a hut at night, but will see that it is sent politely on its way. This, they say, is because their ancestral spirits live underground with the snakes, and emerge at night for a stroll, so no one can be sure that a snake is not some relation. The prohibition against killing snakes does not apply in daytime.

The Dorobo also have a tremendous love of the forest in which they live. They feel respect and friendliness toward the animals that share it with them. As one Dorobo has said: "The Dorobo know the tracks of all the animals, and they like also to see the animals. The animals are not bad, for we all dwell in the forest together. The intelligence of the animals is not like that of people, but it is not very different, for they also are intelligent. Every animal of the forest is alike; we eat some, others we do not; but we like them all. We, and they also, are of the forest."

The Mbuti Pygmies express the most vigorous affection for their forest home. The men refer to it as "mother" and the women call it "father." They are fully aware that the forest provides all their requirements—shelter, food, drink, and security—and that without it they would die. Their entire morality is bound up in the forest, quarrels and other offensive behavior being broken up with the admonition that the forest must not be offended. So closely do the Mbuti identify with their environment that young men have been known to dance alone apparently but actually, they say, with the moon and the forest.

Many other hunter-gatherers have a reverential attitude to plants. The Omaha Indians, for example, always left a pinch of tobacco whenever they picked a plant for its medicinal properties, for they believed that its healing powers were theirs only by the generosity of the plant.

Such attitudes are not confined to hunter-gathers. The Barama River Caribs of Guyana always take care to sprinkle beer on the trees they have to fell when they clear a new garden. They wish to placate the spirits of the trees so

Panare Indians of the Venezuelan forests resting in camp. Familiarity with the forest breeds confidence, not fear.

that they will not skulk malevolently in the surrounding bush but, when the new growth is big enough, will return to guard the swidden.

Perhaps the most complete of any people's identification with its environment is that of the Australian Aborigines. Until destroyed by miners and missionaries, the Aborigines were as much a part of the landscape as the rocks and cliff faces on which they painted their totemic designs.

Among the Wikmunkan Aborigines, for example, every clan had a totem: an animal, plant, or geographical feature with which it was closely associated. Every totem had a sacred spot from which it first originated. These would be bushes, trees, holes, or rocks, generally with water nearby. The killing of an animal or the injuring of a plant near its sacred spot was absolutely prohibited and bound to be followed by misfortune.

The sacred spot was called *auwa*, and ceremonies of increase were held there, when the clan appealed to the spirit of its totem to ensure a plentiful supply of the plant or animal concerned. The clan's senior men painted themselves with designs in white clay representing the totem. The ritual that followed varied according to the totem, but it could include stamping, hitting trees, sweeping the bushes, and making strange noises. In effect, each clan was making itself responsible for the abundance of those objects of economic and social value to the community.

The *auwa* of the bream totem is a small creek running into a major river. It is probably one of the bream's main breeding places. Beside it, ant hills have been arranged in a circle and in lines going east and west from it as if from the *auwa*. Whenever a man from the clan was speared in a fight, it was thought that his spirit went under

Above: Australian Aborigines feel a powerful bond with the rocks and cliffs and other natural features that surround them.

Above: an Aborigine rock painting of a fish totem. Below: Aborigines dancing a totemic dance. The Aborigines had a striking awareness of the unity of man and land, which was expressed in their culture until it was destroyed by Europeans.

water at the bream *auwa*. Another *auwa* was that of the plains turkey. This is a lagoon, and no one was allowed to swim there. Once, a man did so, and as soon as he emerged from the water he died.

It is hard for us to comprehend the deep love and respect the Australian Aborigines had for their totemic sites. All hunter-gatherers have a very close bond with the landscape that is their home and with the animals and plants that share it with them. But only the Australian Aborigines seem to have expressed this bond quite so strikingly—even obsessively—in their rituals and daily life.

Food-collecting survived as a successful way of life for so long because hunter-gatherers have a

highly detailed and comprehensive knowledge of their environment. Many observers, having heard their opinions with scepticism, have been surprised to find how accurate they were.

The explorer Humboldt, for example, when traveling in the Americas was struck by the crocodiles' strange habit of swallowing stones. It is a habit that has often been observed, but until recently was thought quite inexplicable. The Amerindians told Humboldt that the crocodiles retained the stones in their bellies, and this improved their stability and maneuverability under water. Humboldt thought the idea was simply a rather amusing native superstition and did not believe it. But recent research has shown that the Amerindians were right.

One anthropologist, Richard Nelson, was commissioned by the United States Air Force to study Eskimo knowledge of sea ice, the general term for the different types of ice that cover the Arctic sea. If an aircraft is forced to come down in the Arctic, it is essential that its crew know as much as possible about Polar survival techniques. Quite apart from the need to hunt, fish, and keep warm, it is virtually impossible to stay alive without an understanding of how ice behaves. Some ice is as safe as dry land, other ice may crumble or fracture into small floes. One large mass of ice may suddenly break away from another, or equally suddenly they may pack together with crushing force.

Richard Nelson found that the Eskimos could predict, with great accuracy, the likely behavior of the ice on which they were traveling, and that the rules they went by and their descriptions of the physical properties of the ice were of a high scientific standard. They were also expert at remembering their way in what to us is essentially a featureless landscape, and past masters at crossing ice so thin that, were it not for the Eskimos' technique, it would break under the weight of a man. Richard Nelson had some difficulty in believing the Eskimos at first, but in the end he wrote: "Those who live with Eskimos over a long enough period find themselves questioning less, and follow whatever they are told to do by their experienced native companions. It is my opinion that the information given by Eskimos relating to successful hunting or sur-

Eskimos, like all hunting peoples, have a formidable knowledge of animals. Here a group of them are preparing to use the properties of frozen fish for an unusual purpose.

The fish are laid end to end and wrapped in skins previously soaked in water. Before the skins freeze they are trampled into the correct shape. Thus sledge runners are made from frozen fish! The crosspieces are made from caribou bone or antlers. This extreme example of skillful improvization shows how the Eskimos use their knowledge of animals to the full.

Successful hunting demands silence. The otherwise highly voluble Bushmen keep absolutely quiet as soon as they see an animal. They have developed this sign language to tell each other what they have seen. The two-handed gesture above means buffalo. Below are some single-handed signs.

Hawk   Ostrich   Duck

Scrub-hare   Springhaas   Porcupine

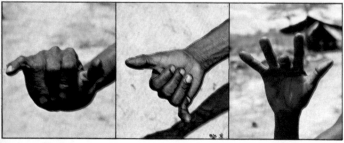

Giraffe   Wart-hog   Lion

vival techniques is nearly always correct and well-founded, regardless of how difficult it may be to accept initially."

Obviously, simply to have survived in such an environment is proof enough of the Eskimos' great knowledge, and this proof applies equally to their knowledge of animals. How else could they have hunted them? Yet many of the peoples who hunt with bow and arrow—for example, the Andamanese, Bushmen, Pygmies, and various Amerindian tribes—are singularly poor shots. At ranges greater than 60 feet or so they are most unlikely to hit their target, and their normal range is about 30 feet. However, their lack of technological competence is amply compensated for by their knowledge of animal behavior. So well do they understand the habits of their prey that they are able to stalk it and get close enough to it to make sure of killing it. By examining tracks, animal droppings, and vegetation that has been bruised or broken when animals have passed by or fed on it, hunting peoples can tell what their prospects are of getting meat that day. In this way, too, they know what species of animal is around, its age, sex, size, and condition, and where it is likely to be. They know the sleeping habits of animals, an obviously advantageous piece of information as there is no easier catch than an animal asleep. At the other end of the scale, some American Indians were able to run down deer by keeping them moving and by taking advantage of their tendency to run in an arc: the hunters simply traversed the shorter distance between the two ends of the arc. By contrast, the modern "sportsman," with his high-powered rifle and telescopic sight, or even with the latest archery equipment, can hunt successfully without even the knowledge to identify his prey by more than a distinction between game and stock.

Knowledge of animals was not confined to their behavior. The Aleuts had an impressive anatomical knowledge, and the multiplicity of uses found by the Eskimos for different parts of an animal is astounding. The blubber, heart, kidney, liver, spleen, and flesh of the northern sea lion, for instance, were eaten as food; the bones were made into clubs, root diggers, and

Above, right: Bushmen pretending to hunt ostriches. Right: Aborigines perform a ritual emu-mimicking dance. Natural man's knowledge of animal behavior often emerges in play and dance.

other tools, depending on their size; the flippers into soles for shoes; the intestines, stomach, and the tube connecting the mouth and stomach (the esophagus) were used for making jackets (the parka), trousers, and pouches; the sinews were used for binding and sewing; the skin as a kayak cover; the teeth as jewelry; the whiskers as decoration for hats; and the pericardium, (the sac enclosing the heart) as a container. The Majangir put the hide alone of an antelope to many uses: carpet, hat, a sling for carrying infants, and sheaths for knives and fire-sticks.

In the past, naturalists and explorers have benefited greatly from hunting peoples' knowledge of animal life, and there is no doubt that serious students of animal behavior still do so. Quite as extensive as his knowledge of animals is natural man's knowledge of plants. We have already gained a great deal from this knowledge, as is shown by a list of plants we eat today which almost certainly we would not have known about if we had not seen them eaten by American

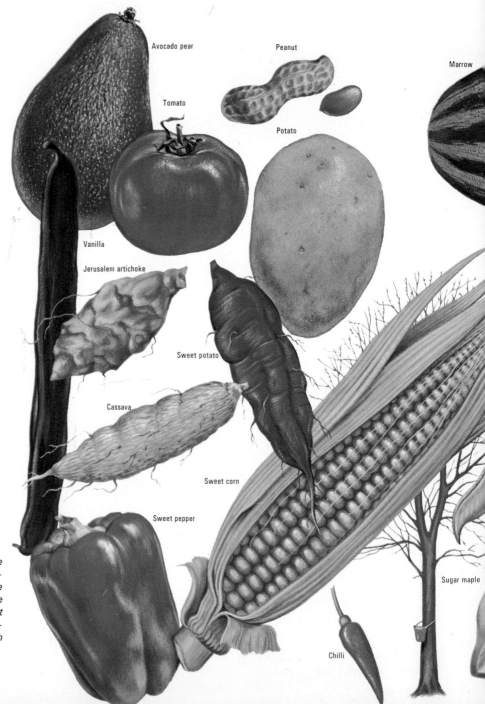

The Amerindians' gift to the world. There are 24 important food-plants that the hungry world would have been without had they not been discovered by the various Indian tribes of South and Central America.

66

Indians: maize (or sweet-corn), sugar maple, peanuts, sunflower seeds, Brazil nuts, cashew nuts, runner beans, french (or kidney) beans, butter beans pineapples, passion fruit, guavas, cocoa, papaya, avocados, marrows, tomatoes, sweet peppers, chilis, vanilla, potatoes, Jerusalem artichokes, manioc (cassava), and sweet potatoes. It can be seen that they include three vitally important staples—maize, manioc (a major food in Africa as well), and potatoes.

It is unlikely that those representatives of natural man still surviving will be able to introduce us to any more major food plants. However, there are probably many of rather more modest importance still awaiting either discovery or wider application. In this latter category are the mongongo nuts of the !Kung Bushmen. This highly nutritious food-plant would be of great value if it could be cultivated in arid lands such as those of Saharan Africa and the Near East. It is also probable that some tropical-forest dwelling tribes know of plants that could be used in

Brazil nuts

Cashew nuts

Kidney bean

Guava

Sunflower seeds

Butter beans

Pineapple

Scarlet runner bean

Cocoa

Papaya

Passion fruit

A Tukano from Peru collects the leaves of the coca plant. Many Amerindian tribes use cocaine and other plant drugs.

beverages. There are plenty of stimulating drinks on the market, but remarkably few genuinely soothing (non-addictive) ones. We are far more likely to discover such a plant by finding it in use among a forest people than by selecting plants at random or by experimenting in laboratories.

From the Amerindians we have also learned about important drug plants such as quinine, cocaine, and curare. Quinine is a well-known antimalarial agent; drugs derived from cocaine are used in dentists' anesthetics; and curare is a drug vital to safe and painless surgery. Cocaine comes from the coca leaf, chewed by the Indians of the Andes, while the many types of curare are various combinations of complex chemical compounds, used by the forest Indians as arrow poisons. It is from their formidable knowledge of such poisons that we are likely to derive most future benefit. A great many fish poisons, for example, remain to be investigated for properties other than their ability to stun fish. Some have already proved useful in bettering our understanding of nerve action. Another is the well-known insecticide Derris. The Barama River Caribs have long known about the insecticidal properties of *haiari*, the plant they use as a fish poison. They treat their tobacco plants with it.

On the other side of the world, the Andaman Islanders use a plant they call *jojonghe* to protect them on their frequent raids of bees' nests. Like many hunting peoples they are extremely fond of honey, and whenever they are about to collect some they smear themselves with *jojonghe* and put some in their mouths. This they chew, breathing the fumes on the bees. The effect is to repel the bees completely, and the honey robbers win their prize absolutely unstung. Only one anthropologist visiting the Andaman Islanders seems to have grasped the usefulness of such a plant. He took some samples of it and planted them in the governor's garden on the main island, so that as soon as they had flowered they could be taken to the mainland of India for identification. Unfortunately, the governor's gardener thought they were weeds and threw them away.

Another branch of natural man's learning of which there is a good deal of evidence but which is almost entirely unexplored, is his knowledge of oral contraceptives and abortifacients. The first are taken before sexual intercourse, the second after. The women of Efate, Gau, and Pentecost, islands in the New Hebrides group, know of a great many plants that they combine to

Some of the uses to which Amerindians put their knowledge of plants. Above left: Tukano Indians cure an after-the-party hangover with green pepper juice. Right: Colorado Indians from Ecuador use a red paste on their hair to repel insects. Below: a Tukano Indian prepares coca leaves. It was from the Amerindians that we learned about cocaine, now used in medicine.

make contraceptives or abortifacients, and that they claim are effective. Their use is a source of friction between the men and the women, for the women want small families while their husbands want large ones. None of the plants used have been tested. Nor have the plants used by the Lesu of New Ireland, which are known only to a few old men who sell the leaves whenever they are required. The situation is further complicated by the refusal of most Lesu women to admit they resort to the plants at all.

Again, it is in South America that research into abortifacient plants is likely to be most successful. The forests of the Amazon-Orinoco basin are rich in a great variety of species, and the Amerindians have a long-standing and intimate acquaintance with them. As we shall see in the next chapter, many of their populations are kept stable through the use of contraceptive and abortifacient plants, the safety of which have been tested by the living laboratories of the tribes themselves.

A fourth group of plants, of which South and Central American peoples in particular have a comprehensive experience, are the hallucinogens, the drugs used to induce trances and visions. As these are normally used in religion and medicine, they will be discussed when we deal with shamanism, in the next chapter.

Finally, natural man employs a wide variety of plants for their different mechanical properties. Besides making common use of gourds of all shapes and sizes for pots, cups, ladles, and dishes, the Majangir also use the bark of a number of vines that they turn into serviceable ropes, and of course they know what wood makes the best fire-sticks. Their houses are made from sticks, grass, and leaves, and are perfectly waterproof. But perhaps they are most skillful in their working of string, carrying bags, and baskets. Their string is made from various plant fibers, by hand of course, but the fibers are bound so well together that they appear manufactured. The carrying bags are made from beaten bark, are very strong, and are most attractive to look at — as indeed are the Majangir baskets, made from different types of cane to which a plant resin is applied to make them waterproof.

Some idea of the food-collectors' general knowledge of plants can be gathered from the fact that their classifications are often more complex than those of Western science. While our classification is based on structure, theirs is based on shape,

Above: Kamayura Indians in the Xingu National Park, Brazil, with bark canoes. Left: a heavily ornamented Eripagtsa mother and daughter. The woman is making a basket of plaited leaves.

taste, smell, and texture. If a botanist wishes to identify a plant he must wait until he sees its flower or fruit, but a hunter-gatherer uses a number of criteria for identification. Nor is his knowledge frozen in time and incapable of modification. The Pinatubo Negritos of the Philippines are—or were until the practice was missionized out of them—constantly improving their knowledge. If they found a plant they did not know, they would taken it home and discuss it with their colleagues.

Farming peoples as different as the Cubeo of Colombia and the Tsembaga of New Guinea have tremendous experimental curiosity and take great delight in trying out new crop varieties.

However, this willingness to experiment is allied with conservatism, and the experimenter will not commit himself to his new variety for many years, until it has been proved better or as satisfactory as the one it might replace. Again it is worth reminding ourselves that very few indeed of our food crops, and none of our major ones, are modern domestications, and it is those areas where the remaining representatives of natural man still live that are most likely to be the centers of the genetic diversity of plant species on which our food supply depends.

So far we have seen that natural man has developed a striking diversity of ways of gaining a living, an intimate and detailed understanding of his environment, and a harmonious relationship with it. All of these things, though essential, would be useless without any capacity to stabilize his population. We know that, in fact, hunter-

!Kung Bushman mother nursing a five-year-old child. Long lactation periods are an important contribution to hunter-gatherer population control. On average lactation periods last for three years, during which time fertility is suppressed.

72

gatherer populations remained virtually stable for a very long time, but until recently it was generally considered that this was because they were subject to starvation and disease of an intensity and frequency only rarely encountered today. Now, however, we know better. Not only do most hunting peoples feed well and easily; they are generally in relatively good health.

Very few full-scale studies of the medical status of pure hunter-gatherers have been carried out. But partial studies, such as that of parasites among Bushmen, reveal that they are much healthier than other, either rural or urban, peoples in the same area. Of the 12 species of parasitic worm found most frequently in rural African populations, only one (the hookworm) was found in Bushmen, and its incidence was not high. The general picture of hunter-gatherer health, life-expectancy, and longevity is that although they are not quite so good as are enjoyed by the average person in the industrialized countries of North America, Europe, Australasia, and Japan, they are much better than can at present be hoped for in the populous non-industrial countries.

It is more than probable that hunting man's health is at least marginally better than that of mixed gardeners and food-collectors—and it is among this latter category that the only full-scale studies have been made. Outstanding among them are those of J. V. Neel and his colleagues on the Xavante of Brazil and the Yanomamo of Venezuela, and Dr. Albert Damon's team from Harvard on the Nasioi and Kwaio peoples of the Solomon Islands.

Dr. Neel described the people he studied as "in general in excellent physical condition," a finding that has been amply borne out by Dr. Damon among the Solomon Islanders. Dr. Damon found that there was a sufficiently large proportion of them old enough for him to do a study on degenerative ailments such as cancer and heart disease so common in the industrial world. Yet such diseases were almost totally absent. In general both studies demonstrate that hunter-gardeners (mixed gardeners and food-collectors) suffer more from infectious and less from degenerative diseases than we do, and that on average they are probably fitter than we are.

Thus it is now accepted by a number of authorities that many hunter-gatherer and hunter-gardener societies stabilize their populations

House on stilts for single men and boys on the Solomon Islands. Separate accommodation for bachelors is a form of population control practiced by some peoples, the efficiency of which is related to the persistence and ingenuity of the young men.

Above: Tasaday men in the Philippines making stone tools. Right: a Tasaday mother with her children. The ability of the tribe to maintain a stable population, as well as the remoteness of their home, must have contributed to their isolation, until discovered in 1971. Now the delicate relationship between themselves and their environment is likely to be destroyed.

deliberately rather than involuntarily through starvation and disease. The means they have adopted are restraint, infanticide, abortion, and contraception. Restraint is practiced in the form of the post-partum taboo, a prohibition on sexual intercourse for up to three years after the birth of a child. This provides at least a minimum of spacing. Infanticide is obvious: the deliberate killing of the child as soon as it is born. It sounds horrible and barbaric to us, but the people who practice it have a good reason for doing so: to them, it is more important that the opportunity of all members of the community to live complete lives is not jeopardized by their having to cope with an excess of numbers. Among the Eskimos, female infanticides were more common than male ones. This is because the men, being hunters, live much more dangerous lives than do the women, and so get killed more easily. If there were as many girls as boys, when they grew up the women would eventually far outnumber the men. Abortion, both direct and by means of abortifacients, and contraception are as common as infanticide, and natural man has a profound knowledge of plants for these purposes, as we saw from the last section.

The mechanics of population regulation among hunter-gatherers and hunter-gardeners are of absorbing interest, but it is still more fascinating to speculate about the controls that stimulate people to resort to these mechanisms. That these controls are powerful is demonstrated by comparing the respective fates of two Amerindian tribes of Brazil, the Tenetehara and the Tapirape. Both tribes lived in virtually identical environments, but the Tenetehara were expansionist and the Tapirape were stable. Tenetehara women left their men if they felt they were insufficiently fertile. By contrast, the Tapirape took care to limit their families to two at most three children, and certainly no more than two children of the same sex. When the white man came to Brazil, both tribes suffered terribly from introduced diseases such as measles and smallpox and from raids by colonists and bandits. Both tribes were decimated, but only one recovered. The Tenetehara continued to be expansionist, their numbers began to increase, until today their population is greater than ever before. The Tapirape, however, continued to regulate their numbers as if nothing untoward had happened. Unfortunately, such control although advantageous for a vigorous

population is disastrous for one that has been reduced to almost nothing—and today the Tapirape tribe is extinct.

This tragic example can be repeated from other tribes. What is the nature of such powerful controls? Nobody knows, and regrettably virtually no research is being conducted on the subject. What is still more confusing is that while the controls appear suicidally powerful among some people, they are highly fragile among others.

The Havasupai, for example, are a small tribe of North American Indians, who live in an enchantingly beautiful canyon in Arizona. During the 200 years for which there are written records, their population has remained stable—except on two occasions. The first was in 1906 after a two-year measles epidemic that halved the population. Interestingly, the population recovered and appeared to stabilize itself. The second occasion occurred with the arrival of a hospital service leading to an expansion of population.

The cause of this rise in population is not that people who formerly would have died from illness are now being saved. It is something quite different. As far as we know, Havasupai numbers were kept down in the past in four ways. The first was a post-partum taboo of two years, and the second was the use of contraceptives, whose effectiveness has not yet been tested. The third was the reduced fertility of the men, as a result of their practice of taking frequent steam baths. It has been suggested that the exposure of the adult men to very hot temperatures, followed by very cold ones when they plunge into the icy stream, lowers fertility by reducing the production of spermatozoa.

The fourth way, and probably the most significant, was abortion. This was a generally accepted way of removing unwanted children, particularly those conceived out of wedlock, until the hospital was built in the locality. Then the Havasupai started having their children in hospital, and abortions virtually ceased. For the first time in their history they had illegitimate children—and a growing population.

By carrying out multigeneration studies of peoples such as the Havasupai, the Tapirape, the Bushmen, and the Andaman Islanders, it may be possible to discover not just new contraceptive drugs, but more significantly what makes a people unconsciously desire to limit its population. For it is only among such people that the answer to this important question can be found.

Havasu Canyon, Arizona, the home of the Havasupai Indians. Until recently, they were able to regulate their numbers so that they remained at peace and could be contained within their cliff-bound home without spreading into the surrounding desert.

Natural Man and his Fellows

Violence is commonly associated with natural man. There are probably two reasons for this. The first is that hunting animals is considered a violent act. We have seen, however, that although finding and killing prey stretch the intelligence and physical prowess of hunters, they hunt with no more aggression than the minimum required to key them up. They certainly feel no aggression toward the animal, and are generally at most reverential, at least neutral.

The second reason is that a society such as ours is fascinated by violence. The anthropological accounts that have greatest impact are the highly colored ones in which the people have strange practices and are particularly violent. Cannibalism, for example, holds a peculiar interest, and is often attributed to a tribe as a regular dietary practice when it is only an occasional ritual one—or not even practiced at all. Thus much more publicity is given to the rather warlike peoples of New Guinea than to the relatively peaceful Semang of Malaya.

Most hunter-gatherers are not at all violent. The !Kung Bushmen have a horror of fighting because, as they say, "someone might get killed," while the Australian Aborigines are exceptionally skilled at ritualizing their aggression. This is not really as surprising as it may sound. Hunter-gatherer bands are small, rarely being larger than 25 people, adults and children. As we shall see, they have little sense of property, and in any case they have nothing worth stealing. Nobody owns land, they simply have the right to hunt animals and gather plants on it. No work is so onerous that anybody would want another person to do it for him. Yet all, both male and female, are needed to do their bit. For these reasons, there is absolutely nothing to gain, either from warfare or from individual acts of violence. Yet of course there is a great deal to lose: life itself, a reduction in the work force, or simply an unpleasant disruption of the community.

A lot of subtle effort is put into preventing such disruption, or smoothing things over when it occurs. There are tensions, in hunter-gatherer communities as there are in ours: one person might feel his share of meat has been inadequate or unfair recently; another might be considered

Many Australian Aborigines ritualized violence, turning potentially dangerous situations into outbursts of fiery rhetoric. Whenever quarrels looked as though they were going to become violent, onlookers would intervene to calm the participants.

by a member of the community not to be pulling his weight; a third might just be going through a patch of surliness and bad temper.

The community will first try to bring the offender into line in such a way as not to make him more aggrieved and aggressive. If he will not be gentled into line, and his behavior seems to be more disruptive than the effects of an open rebuke, then increasingly he will be ostracized by his fellows. Nobody will laugh at his jokes, his questions will go unanswered or be met with irrelevant and totally unsatisfactory replies. All his attempts to make conversation will fail, being met less with silence than with vagueness and indifference. This is not quite the same as putting a person "in Coventry." It is much less obvious and not so overtly hostile. The general idea is to make it clear to the offender that he has done wrong and is publicly disapproved of, but at the

Above: Jalé warriors, New Guinea; the main party watch as their vanguard set fire to a neighboring village. Below: the body of one of the Jalé warriors, killed in ambush.

Jalé warriors, ornamented with shells and bird-of-paradise feathers, celebrating their success with a victory dance.

same time to leave him room for maneuver, an opportunity to pretend that nobody has really noticed, while he turns over a new leaf and makes amends. In other words, there is a general, if subconscious, recognition that if somebody causing disruption is corrected carelessly or heavy-handedly then the disruption will spread and grow; that the wisest course is to make sure that remedial measures are subtle, and reduce the likelihood of further disruption.

If things go wrong and the dispute spreads so that the band is, for example, divided into two opposing factions, then the most likely course is not war but fission. Hunter-gatherer bands are constantly splitting and then coming together again in different combinations of families. Clearly, if one family finds itself temporarily incompatible with another, it is preferable that they go their different ways for a time rather than

foment a full-scale battle between their men. Such fission is the tendency not only among most hunter-gatherers who find no difficulty in moving, but also among hunter-gardeners. For example, the Cubeo of Colombia, like many southern Amerindian peoples, live in communal long-houses, occupied by a number of families. Inevitably, however, for a time one family might not get along with the others. Rather than remaining in the long-house, causing increasing friction until perhaps everybody leaves or somebody resorts to violence, the family will simply abandon the long-house and build a separate hut nearby. Here they will live until the tension subsides.

Aggression is a useful behavior pattern for all species. The problem is to prevent it deteriorating into violence. Most species have developed ways of solving this problem, and natural man is no exception. Here, Chimbu warriors and their women of the New Guinea Highlands are indulging in a harmless war game, which ritualizes, and thus absorbs, excess aggression.

This is not to claim that there are no fights between individuals or battles between groups. If such normally effective controls fail for some reason, armed conflict does break out, sometimes disastrously. The Majangir of Ethiopia are, for the most part, peaceable and friendly. They avoid disputes preferring to laugh off difficulties and differences of opinion. Resentments can smolder beneath the surface, however, only to explode under the influence of too much alcohol. Normally, whenever beer or honey wine is to be consumed, a sufficiently large number of people hear about it for there to be enough to make people merry but not enough to make them uncontrollably drunk. Unfortunately, the system is not entirely foolproof and occasionally the drinking is confined to too few people. Men whose drinking is controlled by scarcity cannot develop self-control, and they then drink far too much. When that happens, and if there is indeed an undercurrent of resentment, then a violent quarrel may break out, all too often ending in the death of one or more of the participants.

Yet on the whole, the violence in hunter-gatherer disputes is effectively ritualized. The Tiwi of northern Australia, for instance, were superficially a violent people. They were given to frequent duels between individuals and battles between groups. The commonest cause of duels was jealousy. The Tiwi marriage system was such that nobody younger than 40 had a wife. This meant that their society consisted of old men with lots of wives, middle-aged men with one or two wives, and young men with no wives at all. The old men were very important, but not much fun for the young women, who also had to bear with the bossiness of the older wives. Thus when all the women went off to gather plants, the temptation for a young man and woman to pass the time in clandestine friendliness was irresistible. The old men knew this, and were therefore constantly accusing their juniors of seduction. This inevitably led to a duel—which consisted of the old man haranguing the young man and then loosing off his spear at him. Because he was not just old but also furious the senior was more than likely to miss his target, so the youth was in little danger. In fact, if he was wise he deliberately allowed himself to receive a small wound so that honor could be satisfied all around.

Group disputes were almost as innocuous. Each individual in the war party spent most of the time haranguing his opposite number, after which everybody threw their spears. The battle ended as soon as somebody was wounded. Sometimes this was fatal, and as often as not the injured party was a spectator; but never was there the kind of slaughter we associate with medieval warfare, modern terrorism, or gang violence.

Wrestling is another way of absorbing excess aggression among the Amerindians. The picture below shows an attack posture, below right, a clinch, and the one on the right, a throw.

Most people's image of leadership among natural man is the splendidly war-bonneted Red Indian chief. But the situation is, of course, much more complicated than that. To begin with a number of societies had no leadership of any kind, and while most hunting peoples did in fact have a head man, his powers were greatly restricted. Furthermore, many American Indian "chiefs" attained their positions simply because their bands were under attack by the white man. The institution of chief was a response to a highly unusual and stressful situation, when it was essential that the mildly anarchic state of affairs that normally pertained among Amerindian communities be transformed into an organization capable of resistance. Indeed, the failure of the Indians to defeat the invaders can be attributed partly to their absurd trustfulness of the white man's good intentions, but largely to their failure to centralize authority under one man. People described as chiefs often had complete control over only a few families, the rest obeying them only in extremely favorable and unusual circumstances. Europeans had the greatest difficulty in understanding this, and rarely did so, which explains their frequent accusations that the chiefs were fickle and treacherous. Even when relations were peaceful, the white men insisted on dealing only with one man, whom they described as chief, because this simplified matters, and was after all the way Europeans conducted their affairs.

Few hunter-gatherer leaders had any great authority, for their societies were truly democratic. It was very rare for a headman not to do his own hunting and fishing, and his wife not to do her own gathering. He had no servants and no special privileges. In fact he was often materially *less* well off than his fellows. He derived his authority from his prestige, and prestige was won in a number of different ways, a particularly important one being generosity. The ethic of not hoarding, together with that of sharing, are very important among hunter-gatherers. It follows that to gain prestige a man had to be even more generous than the norm. One anthropologist leaving the tribe he was living with was grateful enough to the chief to present him with an antelope he had shot. Somewhat embarrassed, the

A typical image of tribal leadership: the Northern American Indian chief. Often, however, the chief emerged only in response to the new, threatening situation caused by the arrival of the white man.

The African chief is another popular image of tribal authority. The chief shown here is Winyi IV, Omukama of Bunyoro, in Uganda.

chief refused the gift, asking the anthropologist to give it to somebody else, lest the jealousy of the band be aroused against him.

Prestige is also won by skills such as hunting, by a sense of humor, and by an ability to smooth over disputes. If there is a quarrel and the headman does not settle it, he is likely to be roundly abused by some of his people. If he intervenes too obtrusively he will be attacked by the disputants for being overweening and authoritarian! It would be surprising, therefore, if headmen really enjoyed their position, and, indeed they have few rivals for the job. It is perhaps because of this that succession to leadership is usually by birth.

This does not mean that there are "royal families" among hunter-gatherers. If the head-

man dies his son or brother may replace him; but only if his fellows regard him as suitable. The authority of a headman is limited to advice, which is usually followed because of his prestige. But if his people think little of him, he will be utterly ignored, and will soon relinquish his position to someone else. Among the Cubeo, for example, it is the responsibility of the chief to see that the communal house is built. The Cubeo are not hunter-gatherers, relying to a large extent on gardening as well as hunting and fishing, but they illustrate a principle common among truly food-collecting peoples, The *maloca,* which is what the communal long-house is called, normally lasts for about five years. When a new one must be built, the headman will set up the main beams with his brothers and sons. At that point, if they still approve of him, the rest of the men in the community will join in and help. However, if for

Above: Winyi IV receives his tribal elders in the royal compound, and below, the Bunyoro royal trumpeters blowing their sacred horns covered with cowrie shells. Such authority and its trappings within a tribe are absent among hunting peoples.

some reason he no longer commands respect, none of the other men will bother. This will be a clear sign to him that he should give way to somebody else, which he will do.

His replacement will probably be one of his sons or brothers, though it could also be somebody from outside his family. The reason why the new leader is more likely to be from the old leader's family, is that a son or close male relation will tend to model his behavior on that expected of a chief. Thus he will already have acquired prestige by showing what a generous and moderate man he is. Whoever he is, he will be the community's choice, because the people can clearly demonstrate to any prospective leader whether or not he can expect their co-operation.

This system, in a way rather like the four-yearly presidential elections in the U.S.A., is plainly an effective way for the community to keep its leader up to the mark. In the case of a man becoming chief on the old leader's death, a new house must be built, however new the existing one is; and this, too, is obviously an excellent way of demonstrating whether or not he is acceptable.

Apart from the single, rather restricted, position of the leader, communities of natural man have no hierarchy or class system. This is possible firstly because wealth does not flow in the direction of authority, as it does in our society—and in fact the wealth, such as it is, flows away from authority. Secondly, the communities are very small, which means they can be truly democratic. When everybody knows everybody else, when expertise is shared, and when there is plenty of time to discuss things fully, then it can be guaranteed that decision-making will be democratic. This means that it is extremely difficult for a hierarchy or class to be established. As soon as any individual or group tries to dominate, the rest of the community resorts to the usual sanctions to prevent it.

This is not to say that communities were completely unstructured. Apart from kinship alliances, which will be described in a later section, a number of peoples had special groupings—such as the dyadic partnerships of the Netsilik Eskimos. These consisted of two men getting together and agreeing to be trading partners, or to share names, or to exchange wives. The function of these partnerships was probably to reinforce loyalty in an environment hostile enough to make community cohesion of the utmost importance.

But on the whole, natural man has little need of institutionalized community cohesion. There is little difficulty in getting food and everybody knows how to, so that only the old, the infirm, and the very young have a genuine physical need for others. Hence the tendency to fission and the marginal authority of the headman. Thus, what the headman can give his people is limited to his experience and his capacity to resolve conflicts, which is not to say that these qualities are not highly important. This extreme flexibility and reduced central power is valuable in that it

Men building a longhouse. Among southern Amerindians it is the job of the headman to organize house-building, and it is a sign of his unacceptability if he receives no cooperation.

minimizes the possibility of inter-band battles, although of course this makes the community correspondingly vulnerable when faced with a strongly centralized enemy.

Religion is probably the area of natural man's life about which it is most difficult to generalize. It is also the least easy to understand. Religion is not a separate compartment of natural man's experience as it often is of ours. It is the expression of all his values, of his total world-view. Few hunting peoples have any conception of a single God, one creator of the universe, or if they have they are not much concerned about him. They are animists, populating the world about them with spirits, some good, others bad. The Majangir of Ethiopia, for example, believe in a rainbow spirit, which is both good and bad. Good because it stops excessive rain, but bad simply by virtue of its tremendous power. All creatures have power, the Majangir believe, but something with very great power, such as a strong spirit, is dangerous to something that is relatively weak such as an ordinary man. Power is comparable to heat. Human beings have an average blood temperature of about 98°F, and if they were exposed to a heat source of say 298°F they would be completely consumed. This in effect is what is said to happen when a Majangir is exposed to the rainbow spirit: he falls ill with a fever, and will probably die. Fortunately, the tribal chief and his male relatives, because of *their* power, are able to force the rainbow spirit away whenever it is encountered, thus protecting their people.

Men (and women) with unusual knowledge of the spirit world are known as shamans or medicine men. They are the exceptions to the generalization that there are no specialists among hunter-gatherers and hunter-gardeners. Everybody knows something of ritual and the medicine with which it is associated, but the shaman knows a great deal more than anybody else. Again there are exceptions even to this rule; for the Bushmen have no shaman, most of the men being capable of joining in the medicine dance and other religio-medical activities.

Perhaps the most interesting shamans are those of the Indians in Central and South America, for they have a most impressive knowledge of hallucinogenic drugs. These they will use by smoking or chewing them, or having them blown with painful force as a snuff up their nostrils. The best known example of such a shaman

Top: a Navaho (northern Amerindian) shaman at work. First, a ritualized design is "painted" with colored powders in the sand. Next, above, the shaman scatters corn (maize) as an offering to the spirits, so that they will help him cure the patient.

is Don Juan. This "man of knowledge" of the Yaqui tribe of northern Mexico is still alive. He is highly skilled in the use of three hallucinogenic plants—peyote, jimson weed, and the psilocybe mushroom. Because he knows them so well, he can use them to experience a completely different reality to the natural one known by us. It is a world of dreams and hallucinations, a world that we would find highly unreal. Once

Above: the completed painting in the sand. Round it are baskets of colored powders, and prayer sticks, and rattles. Below: the shaman sings his invocations, while his patient sits inside the sacred picture area so that the spirits can cure her.

inside it, however, its reality and its great beauty and power are overwhelming. It is also extremely dangerous. Only an expert like Don Juan knows how to control the effects of the drugs he takes, or to cope with the events of this other reality, which to the novice are quite terrifying. Unless the drugs are taken under supervision of a shaman as part of the long and difficult task of being a shaman apprentice, they are more often than not killers.

The use of trance by shamans is the commonest way in which they communicate their power and special knowledge. Outside the Americas hallucinogenic plants are not widely used to induce trance. More general are the self-induced trances, such as those of the Bushmen in their medicine dances. The shamans are skilled at hypnotizing themselves into trance, or they may be peculiarly sensitive to certain stimuli that help them go into a trancelike state. Some shamans have neurotic tendencies, which the community has sensibly socialized by giving them the opportunity to become shamans.

Many shamans resort to tricks and dramatic devices to help their patients to be fully responsive to their treatment. The intention of such tricks is not to deceive, they are not "mumbo-jumbo," but more the equivalent of the Western doctor's bedside manner or the placebo pills given to people just to satisfy them that they are being properly looked after. The Comanche shamans

Above: a Karaja man who has scarified his body cleans the blood off his skin. Scarification is often done ritually, but also frequently out of vanity. Right: Kamayura flute players in Brazil praying for an end to the rainy season, so that they can start fishing again. The women are not allowed to hear the flutes being played, for they are regarded as very sacred.

Above: a Kraho shaman of Brazil curing a child. He sucks out evil and blows in good, a practice that survives among us when we "kiss things better." Left: a southern Amerindian inhaling a hallucinogenic snuff. Such drugs are used with great expertise by shamans to assist communication with spirits.

Amerindian totem poles such as these near Ketchikan, Alaska, were common among the peoples of the northern Pacific coast.

used to work in pitch darkness. With the aid of drums and the curious noises they could make from different parts of the tent (they were highly effective ventriloquists), they induced the patient and his relations to believe that the sickness was caused by a monstrous demon, and that the shaman was grappling with it. As the fight proceeded both patient and audience were driven to a climax of terror, followed by exquisite relief as the shaman vanquished his opponent. This invariably had a remarkable psychological effect on the patient, whose belief that he was now past the crisis point significantly aided his recovery.

Among the Australian Aborigines, religion and the activities of the medicine man were largely expressed through totemism. In order for the medicine man's power to be effective he had to develop a particularly close relationship with an animal. It was generally believed that he worked with the help of or through the totemic animal, in other words that the animal actually acted for him. Because the relationship was so intimate, the medicine man would not eat his totemic animals, and they in turn protected him.

The possession of totems was not confined to medicine men. Everybody had one; and in southeast Australia there were special sex-totems, representing the sex division in each tribe and emphasizing solidarity within the sexes. Among the Worimi tribe the men's totem was the bat, and the women's the woodpecker. If the men hurt or insulted the women's totem, or vice versa, there would be a violent quarrel or even a fight. This sexual totemism was allied to the belief that men and women had different ancestral origins.

There were also special totems for clans and other divisions within tribes. Members of a clan regarded themselves as related to their totemic animal as much as they were to the other human members of their clan. Such totemism has two important functions. The first is a social one, whereby the bond with people believed to have descended from the same ancestor is reinforced. The second is a natural one, whereby the individual is strongly and persistently reminded of his dependence on the rest of the natural world.

The totem was not necessarily an animal. It could just as well be a plant, a rock, a spring, a cliff, or any other natural feature. Reverence would be expressed toward the totem in a number of different ways: either by refraining to eat or injure the animal or plant; or by a dance associated with it; or by painting designs descriptive

An Australian Aborigine painted with totemic animals.

of it or actually on it if it was a physical feature such as a cliff. These designs were, and sometimes still are, major art forms in their own right, and the Aborigines are justly famed for them.

Clan totemism was, broadly speaking, of three types: matrilineal, patrilineal, and "geographical." A matrilineal clan was one whose members were related to the mother's line. A patrilineal clan was one whose members were related by the father's line. And a geographical clan one whose members depended not on relationship but on the totemic site nearest to which they were born or conceived. The function of matrilineal totems was social reinforcement. The function of patrilineal and "geographical" totems was the promotion of spiritual beliefs and of the cult-life. It was around such totems that the activity known as dreaming was centered.

The dreamtime is eternal, both past and present at once. In the dreamtime, the great heroes of the past are still alive, and their totems are alive

and part of them too. Dreaming is, therefore, an action that is not controlled by restrictive notions of time and space. A man who is a member of such a totem is strictly enjoined to preserve and keep secret the myths, rites, and sacred totem sites, and to hand them on to his son. Membership of a patrilineal or a "geographical" clan is thus equivalent to membership of a secret society.

The lack of preoccupation with personal property is one of the main distinguishing features between natural man and ourselves. Land, the means of production, is never owned by hunter-gatherers. Anybody can hunt, fish, and gather wherever he or she likes. There are restrictions, but these are not imposed because anyone owns anything, but out of a general recognition of what is best for the community. For example, under the guidance of their headman a Bushman band will probably discuss where the women should gather plants in order to get the highest return without straining the long-term capacity of a particular area to supply them. And the Sanpoil of Canada appointed a Salmon Chief to ensure the fish were harvested in the best way.

Instead of land ownership people have usufructory rights, the rights to the fruits of the land. Once a root has been dug up, a fish caught, or an animal shot, then it is owned by somebody. However, the owner cannot do what he wishes with it. Generally, plants and very small animals, such as rabbits or birds, are shared only among the family, although if anyone else is hungry he will not be refused. However, large animals—anything bigger than a small antelope—are shared throughout the entire band.

There is an elaborate system for the division of meat, which varies from people to people, but a typical one is that of the !Kung Bushman. Although the meat "belongs" to one person he does not really own it but is responsible for initially sharing it out among the men who were on the hunt. These men will then further divide their share among relations and people from whom the family has received meat in the past. Often the "owner" of the meat will have the privilege of having a choice cut—for instance the liver or the rump—but whenever a large animal is killed everybody will get some meat. The only thing that really varies each time an animal is caught is the distribution route on which each joint actually travels.

One obvious reason why only the larger animals are shared is that it is impossible for a single family to consume them unassisted. They could of course attempt to do so over a few days, but the meat might go bad before they have

Left: Dobe !Kung Bushmen hang strips of meat and (center) a Dyak of Borneo lays out venison to dry. Right: Nyae Nyae !Kung Bushmen share out a meal. Meat preserving and meat sharing are common practices among most hunting peoples.

All the items on this page are considered by the Bushmen to be personal possessions, but they are still readily shared. Above: a Bushman playing the Bushman "violin." Right: a man applies poison to his arrows. Below: simple storage utensils, such as these pots, bowls, and ladles, are made from gourds.

finished it. In any case, any attempt to keep so much would be disastrous: it would provoke a great deal of ill-feeling and be an open invitation to theft. This of course is the main reason why meat is so scrupulously shared. For, although meat is more perishable than plant foods it can be kept for a while, even in the tropics: the Ethiopian Majangir char and lightly smoke their meat so that it is still perfectly edible after a week. But without meat-sharing there would be little material incentive for people to form communities (although there would still be psychological ones), nor any point in a code of morality which regarded stealing as so reprehensible that only a social outcast would practice it.

In most communities of natural man, in fact, theft is virtually unknown. No doubt this is in large part due to the size of these communities. They are so small that everybody knows what everybody else is doing, and they can even identify footprints. There is thus a practical disincentive to stealing: it is impossible to avoid

An Amerindian woman making a hammock. Hammocks are not considered common
property. This does not cause any problems because all women are able to make them.

being detected. Because theft is so improbable, it is considered as serious a crime as murder.

Apart from food, there is not much that natural man can own. There are clothes, which are generally never more than a leather cloak, and often as little as a belt for holding leaves or grass; and there are weapons and cooking pots, all easily replaceable items. Finally, there are ornaments and other objects of aesthetic value, including musical instruments. Often a true sense of ownership can be attributed only for those objects absolutely essential to survival. Generally, however, the property values relating to food apply to the other items as well. It is wrong to hoard, it is good to share. If someone asks for something, he must be given it. Possessions such as these move from one person to a great many others because it is considered anti-social to refuse a request for any of them.

Some agricultural peoples have similar attitudes to property as have hunter-gatherers. For example, among the Lesu of New Ireland, land is not owned by anybody until it is first cleared. A man has the right to clear a garden at any place where none has existed. As soon as it is cleared it is owned, and no one may take any of the produce without the owner's permission. The principle of reciprocity—exchanging goods and services over a period of time—is also well established. Among the Bomagai-Angoiang of New Guinea this extends to the giving of gardens or parts of gardens to other women besides the wife. The idea is that the man clears a plot and then gives it to his wife in exchange for the produce grown in it. But he also gives plots to his sisters and to widows. The advantage of this system is obvious: food production is more assured because it is less likely to be subject to poor planning, or

Sweet-potato cultivation in New Guinea. Gardens such as this are private property when they are cleared.

to a single woman's wrath during a marital dispute; and because different gardens will be planted by different women at different times, so that as one is exhausted another is ready for harvest. The same principle applies when one man gives a pig to another. He knows that sooner or later he will be given a pig in return, probably when he is more in need of one. And in the meantime he does not have the bother of looking after a troublesomely large herd, or preventing the pig breaking up his or his neighbor's garden.

Reciprocity means that nobody goes uncared for. Old people who have looked after their children will be cared for by them in return. It also ensures social cohesion. In theory it would be possible for a single family to be totally self-supporting, but people need company as well as food, and they also need long-term insurance against disaster. By exchanging goods and services between them, families build up a series of obligations and rights that cement them into a community. Because they can support themselves, families can temporarily leave the community when tensions become unbearable. On the other hand, because they are obliged to return any gifts made to them by others, and are also owed gifts in return for the ones they themselves have given, they are bound to come back. Thus, the combination of fission and reciprocity provides the community with optimum flexibility and cohesion.

Among some peoples the principle of reciprocity has built up into an elaborate exchange cycle that extends over thousands of miles. For example, the best stone axes came from a certain part of Australia while other parts boasted particularly fine ochers and dyes for painting. Consequently these localized valuables often traveled great distances between tribes and bands of one region and another. No economic class of tradesman was established, however, since reciprocal arrangements assured that each trading partner was obliged not to hang onto his property: there was always somebody he owed something to.

Status is knowing where you stand in relation to your fellows. Status, and the striving for prestige in order to improve status, are very old. All societies of natural man, and probably all societies, share this concept. Natural man values status rather more than possessions. There is no indication of status among his possessions, as

A Corroboree, or Aborigine trade and exchange ceremony, in Arnhem Land, Australia. Trade in items such as stone axes and paints and dyes once extended from tribe to tribe right across the continent.

The proud headdresses of New Guinea warriors and rich orna-
mentation of the tribesmen are signs of status. Killing another
man rarely confers status among hunting peoples.

there is in our society. On the contrary, as we
have already seen, the reverse is the case, a man's
status depends in large measure on his generosity
in giving away his possessions.

This is not true of all hunting peoples. For
example, the Indians of the Northwest coast of
America amassed prestige through wealth and
even kept slaves. However, they are exceptional:
in general, hunter-gatherers find other ways of
gaining prestige, and the system rarely becomes
hierarchical. There is no ranking order from
people with high status to people with low status.
People remain equal, whatever their status, so

that a man will enjoy great esteem without gaining any privileges or even any obvious sign of respect from his fellows. The main differences in social relations between a man with little prestige and a man with a lot is that the latter's advice on matters about which he is esteemed will be listened to carefully and probably followed; and his fellows will be more favorably disposed toward him.

Prestige can be won by a person performing the role expected of him, to the best of his ability. The man who takes care over his hunting, fishing, weapons-making, garden-clearing, or house-building will be respected. So will the woman who diligently gathers or grows plants, makes a good home, and so on. The person who plays music, or carves ornaments, or in any other way harmoniously fulfills his role in the community will be in good standing with it. Whoever works hard and is generous, whoever is good-humored and friendly, in other words whoever boosts community morale whenever he or she can, will enjoy high status. On the other hand, anyone who is lazy, mean, grumpy, and ill-disposed toward his fellows will be shunned.

A skilled hunter, who brings large supplies of meat into the community, will be very much respected, although again, he will not be considered superior to one less lucky or adept. Indeed, his success will be attributed less to his skill than to his obviously harmonious relationship with the animals. Since it is believed that you must respect animals or they will simply not be there to be killed, it follows that a successful hunter must have a good relationship with his prey. Thus he will be in harmony with his en-

Prestige is won by fulfilling one's role as well as possible. Among the Makuna people of Colombia, one male role is that of boat-maker. The boats are made from tree trunks. First the bark is removed, then the tree is hollowed out and this process is accelerated by burning. The craft is then shaped with fire and chisel and finally launched.

vironment, and he will be of high moral stature. Accordingly, he will be valued as a "good" man rather than as a "clever" one.

This does not mean that there are no powerful men within these small communities. Some will have stronger personalities than others. They may have greater oratorical skill, or be better hunters, or harder workers. Particularly among hunter-gatherers it will be possible to accumulate more and thus be more generous and consequently still more influential. Among the Majangir, for example, the size of your garden depends on the number of men you can attract to help you clear it. This depends on the amount of obligation you have built up in your favor—by providing meat and especially by providing honey wine. The provision of honey wine in turn depends on the number of hives you have. The hives are made from hollowed-out logs and are placed high up in trees. Making and placing them is extremely hard work and it is best to get help. But help will only come from those obliged by your generosity to give it to you!

If a man wishes to enjoy great prestige he must have more than his fellows to be generous with, He must therefore work very much harder. An exceptionally hard worker will have a larger garden and theoretically it should be possible for him to pass this on to his children, thus creating something like a system of large landowners among relatively impoverished peasants. This does not happen because of the key role of generosity in the winning of prestige. The "richer" and more influential a Bomagai-Angoiang "big man" is, the more he must give away. He will support widows and orphans without expecting them to pay him back. He will even give away parcels of his land without expecting any of the fruits of that land. The more he gives without strings, the greater his prestige. Because Bomagai-Angoiang "big men" give so much away they have, if anything, a keener sense of property than most, because unless you own you cannot give. But at the same time there is the clear recognition that if a few people own too much, the differential will destroy the whole system. Consequently, if a man has an unusually large number of pigs, his clansmen will resort to sorcery to make them sicken and die. Thus, there is no distinction between rich and poor, and status is a means of distributing wealth as well as conferring dignity.

The family is at the heart of community life and natural man is no exception in this respect. But the family means different things to different people. Among one people, for example, an uncle on your mother's side might be referred to as "father," or cousins be considered as brothers and sisters. This just means that kin terms such as mother or son reflect social rather than biological reality.

Human beings differ from other animals in that their offspring are weak and helpless for very much longer. The family is necessary to support and train children, and to equip them for adult life in their society. Social relations are more important than biological ones, and many kinship structures implicitly recognize this: as long as there are enough people responsible for looking after some aspect of the child's life, it does not much matter whether they are actually related. We have something similar to this in our society in the institution of the godparent. The godparents are responsible for the spiritual welfare of their godchild. In another society, they might be called simply father and mother, so that the child has two of each, and be responsible for other aspects of the child's well-being.

Tasaday families. This newly discovered people will have much of interest to add to our knowledge of family life.

Kin terms like father and mother formalize and strengthen the relationship. In many societies this principle is extended throughout the community, so that whenever one person has anything to do with another they both know exactly how they *relate* to each other, which is all that "relationship" means. This has the advantage of defining precisely what kind of behavior is expected: whether extreme formality, or casual joking; affection, or reserve.

Kin terms also define the obligations of those people to each other. Everybody is then clear who is expected to support whom in times of crisis, and who is obliged to give priority to whom before sharing with anybody else, and so on. This arrangement serves as an intimate version of the welfare state. Old people and orphans will not go without while they have at least some form of kin relationship with someone in the community. Indeed, among most hunter-gatherer peoples there are no orphans—except in the strict biological sense—as they quickly become part of other families. Old people are well cared for, too.

Because the function of the family is to provide support, a prospective husband's ability to look after his wife and provide meat for her family is the most important quality they will look for. Of course, as their communities are small they will know quite a lot about his character already. It is unusual for a marriage to be considered unsuitable by the parents of either party, since they would have had ample time to make it clear beforehand that the liaison was looked on with disfavor. Nonetheless, it is normal for a young Bushman, for example, to live with his wife's parents and to hunt for them. If during this period he proves himself a poor hunter he might be thrown out.
There is plenty of leeway in the matter, because, as among many hunting peoples, a couple is not considered married until the girl is pregnant. The logic of this is that marriage and the family exist in order to provide security for children, and if no baby is expected there is no point in them. This gives considerable scope for premarital experimentation.

The Mbuti Pygmies of Zaire have an interesting betrothal festival called the *elima*. The *elima* is partly a puberty rite for girls. As soon as a girl has menstruated for the first time, she is eligible for this rite. The young girls spend some time confined together in a hut where they are instructed in contraception, abortion, sexual intercourse, childbirth, and so on, by the older women. The *elima* lasts from one to two months, and during this time each girl is entitled to leave the hut regularly to whip the boy of her choice—if she can catch him. If she does, he must enter the hut with her, and if she gives him permission, make love with her. After a while the lovemaking ceases to be by invitation only, and the boy may enter the hut whenever he likes—as long as he can successfully get past the older women, all armed with sticks and stones with which they bombard him. Although all boys suffer this treatment, the women aim more particularly at those they regard with least favor. This effectively stops anybody the women regard as unsuitable. During the last two weeks, if the boy is still with the same girl, he is considered betrothed to her and must stay with her. Once the *elima* is over, the young man must prove himself a good hunter, and as soon as he has done so, the couple may live together. Again, however, they are not regarded as married, until she becomes pregnant.

Divorce is generally simple among hunting peoples. If a couple ceases to get on, they part. If a woman feels she is not being adequately looked after by her husband, she will return to her father; and if a man feels his wife is not fulfilling her duties, he returns her to her father. But after an initial period of instability in the early years, most marriages become stable.

Child-rearing among natural man is characterized by considerable physical contact initially, a minimum of corporal punishment, and the use of example as the only educational strategy.

The most obvious physical contact that the infant has from birth is with his mother's breast. Hunter-gatherer and hunter-gardener children are fed at the breast for an average of two and a half to three years. The minimum period recorded being one year and the maximum six years. This does not meant that they are fed exclusively from the breast. Quite early on they are introduced to supplementary foods, usually exactly the same food as that eaten by the adults. The only difference is that the child's food is chewed up for him by his mother before she gives it to him. This practice might be regarded as grossly un-

Pygmy children spend most of their time with their elders and are, therefore, involved in all the various camp activities.

hygenic, but in fact it is just the opposite. The small number of germs transmitted to the child in this way give it immunity against disease. Studies among the Yanomamo of Venezuela have demonstrated that because of their contact with low-level populations of germs from food and from the dirt of hut floors and so on, children have as high a level of antibodies in their blood as United States children do after vaccination.

Normally, the child is given the breast on demand; and the readiness to feed infants in this way not only increases resistance against disease, but also gives them a tremendous sense of security. The most casual observation of very young mammals shows how much they need to be close to their mother, or some similar body—to be enveloped in physical warmth. Humans are no exception, and the highly physical response of hunter-gatherer women to their small children is a major contribution to the sense of security with which they grow up. Whenever a child cries it is given the breast, and until it has learned to toddle

it is always in someone's arms—if not its mother's, then those of its father, another adult, or an older child.

Among the Lesu of New Ireland in the Pacific, as soon as the child can toddle, the care of it is divided between various members of the family. The father will sit for hours on end playing with his children at home or on the beach. Small children are fondled a great deal by other adults besides the parents, yet they do not appear at all spoiled. Generally they are models of cheerfulness, crying only when hungry. After about the age of three they are not fondled nearly so much, however. They are treated with great affection but nobody coos over them any more. Their time is divided between their parents and children of their own age.

Bushmen parents are very indulgent, spending a great deal of time with their small children. The young ones remain with the woman, but as they grow older the children spend increasing amounts of time with adults of their own sex, learning by example their future role in life. The Bushmen resort to corporal punishment very rarely indeed. If they have a difficult child, they just make sure he is constantly in the company

A Waura Indian mother and child in Brazil. Amerindians, like most tropical hunting peoples, are indulgent toward children.

of an adult who will break him in, though not beat him.

The Siriono of Bolivia also enjoy passing the time playing with their children, and like the Bushmen, they rarely resort to physical punishment, preferring instead to shout at offenders. Among hunting peoples—particularly in tropical and subtropical environments—nonviolence is in fact the rule for the upbringing of children as much as it is for adult relationships. Hunter-gatherer parents tend to be harsher in colder lands, where possibly discipline needs to be enforced to a greater extent if people are to survive. This generalization applies only to hunter-gatherers and it is not claimed that latitude is by any means the only regulating factor or even the most significant one.

Education, also, is very similar among all hunting peoples. It is by involvement. Just as small infants have a lot of physical contact with adults, so children as they grow out of infancy continue to have a great deal of social contact

!Kung Bushmen mothers relax with their children. Bushmen adults spend much time playing with and cuddling infants.

with adults. Most of their time is spent with their elders, not because they are being looked after by them, but because it is considered normal and proper for children to be a part of all experience. They are not excluded from anything in which the adults normally take part.

Thus by the time they are about 10 years old, and often long before that, hunter-gatherer children will have done all the things their parents do—hunting, fishing, gathering, gossiping, and so on. Consequently they will already have a good idea of what plants and animals are good to eat or are useful for various other reasons. They will also know those that are poisonous, or dangerous in other ways. They may have known hunger, and they will certainly have eaten their fill after watching animals killed, butchered, and shared out. They will probably have seen their parents get drunk, and may well have seen them or some other couple make love. They may also have watched the birth and perhaps death of babies. It must be borne in mind,

Above: children watch a Solomon Islander carve a model canoe, and below, an Aborigine shapes a club. Left: an Aborigine mother and her children gather mussels. As they grow older, children spend an increasing amount of time with an adult of their own sex, thus learning their future role in the community.

however, that many hunting peoples do not have alcohol and a number are secretive about love-making and birth. Nevertheless very early on, the hunter-gatherer child will have seen more of life than a good many Europeans and Americans will ever see in their lifetimes. And at the same time, they will be learning their roles in life, how to play their parts in supporting themselves and the community. A small boy will be given a small bow, and with it he will shoot grasshoppers, graduating to rabbits and birds, until he is

capable of taking small antelope. He will learn how to butcher an animal, so that the skin is not ruined and no part of the animal is wasted.

A small girl will learn how to find and prepare plants, how to cook, possibly how to weave, and certainly how to sew. Besides basic skills such as these, both boys and girls will learn the customs, the traditions, the entire way of life of their people. They will not be instructed in them, but will simply pick them up through being totally steeped in them. Not all of them will be with adults for much of their time, however. Among some peoples, the boys go around in play packs; they fish and hunt together, and otherwise act as a junior version of the group formed by their fathers and the other men. In such cases, they are imitating the adults as a body rather than as individuals.

The period in a Western child's development that parents dread most is adolescence "the difficult stage." The children of hunting peoples do not appear to experience adolescence in quite so severe a form. They grow from boys and girls to men and women much more smoothly and rather more quickly. This is not because they mature physically much more quickly—normally the reverse is true. It is because by the time they reach puberty, they already know a good deal about how their environment and their community work. And although they still have a lot to learn they are allowed to do so as adults and not as part children, part grown ups.

The changeover from childhood to adulthood is usually marked by a puberty rite, although no one is regarded as truly adult until he or she is married. One such puberty rite—for girls—was described in the last section. An example of one for boys is the *aka-op* ceremony of the Andaman Islanders. The boy must dance all night until daybreak, when he goes into the sea for a couple of hours or so. Afterwards, he kneels on the ground in the open to have his back scarified. An older man takes an arrow and cuts three vertical rows of incisions in the boy's back. Each row consists of 20 to 30 cuts. When that is over, the boy sits with his back to the fire until the blood

clots. Throughout the entire operation and for some hours afterwards the boy must remain completely silent.

As soon as the wounds on his back are healed, a similar operation is performed on his chest. During the entire period, certain foods are forbidden him. These foods are normally staples so they are not all prohibited at once. To begin with, if he is a member of one of the coastal tribes, he is forbidden turtle, dugong, porpoise, various grubs, fish, shellfish, birds and a great many plant foods. When the men decide he can resume eating turtle and the other foods, they hold a turtle-eating ceremony. They kill a large number of turtles, and when they are ready they seat the boy on special leaves, facing the sea. The master of ceremonies then picks up some meat and fat of cooked turtle, takes them to the boy, and rubs his entire body with the fat. He then covers the boy's body in iron oxide, and feeds him with some of the turtle. The boy is then vigorously massaged, after which he is sprinkled with water and clay.

At this point, the boy is allowed to eat unassisted. But he may eat only turtle, and then only with a wooden skewer, because he must not touch the meat with his hands, and drink only water. And for two days and two nights he is not allowed to lie down, speak, or sleep. Some of the men and women talk and sing to him to keep him awake. On the third day, a belt and necklace made from a vine are put on him, and he is allowed to sleep. Later he can wash in the sea, after which various designs in red paint and white clay are painted on him. On the fourth day, the boy and the men helping to initiate him dance until the boy is exhausted. This dancing is repeated for the two following days, at which point the turtle ceremony ends.

The boy can now eat turtle, but is forbidden pork. Eventually he is allowed to eat pork and resume a normal life, but only after a pig ceremony as intricate and prolonged as the turtle ceremony. It is clear from this that the importance of the transition from boyhood to manhood is indelibly impressed on the boy. The rite is probably alarming and certainly fatiguing. It is almost inevitable that he will emerge much changed: no longer a child, but well on the road to experienced adulthood.

Above: a boy emerges after his initiation into the men's house. Below: Jalé dancers outside a men's house.

A young Kamayura girl emerges after months of enforced puberty seclusion, one of the ways of preparing for adulthood.

Natural Man meets Urban Man

As soon as a significant proportion of the human species ceased to live in a stable relationship with their environment, it was probably inevitable that the existence of natural man would be gravely imperiled. However few in numbers the expansionists were at first, they were bound in the end to outnumber those that remained stable. No doubt it was also inevitable that the expansionists should not only take over natural man's land but also *feel* a bitter hostility toward him.

The treatment of natural man by urban man is probably the most despicable aspect of our civilization. Hunter-gatherer and hunter-gardener peoples have been raped, murdered, and exterminated; they have been tortured, humiliated, and enslaved. Whether for trade, conquest, greed, colonial aggrandisement, or the good of heathen souls, natural man has been either utterly demoralized or else driven to extinction.

The relationship between urban man and natural man is most fully illustrated in the plight of the Amerindians, especially those of the United States and Brazil. Today, peoples who once roamed free over a continent are now confined

The primitive log cabin of a modern northern Amerindian.

118

The interior of such a hut. These structures express the cultural limbo in which the Indians now live.

The wretchedness of dwellings such as this Eskimo hut reflects both the poverty and the loss of a way of life.

to about 200 reservations in 26 States of the U.S.A. These reservations vary in size, from the graveyard of the Mohawks—a few acres, large enough for the Mohawks to occupy only when they are dead—to the nine million acres of the Navahos in Arizona. They vary in quality, too, from lakeside woodland, as in Minnesota, to Arizona's desert.

Some 450,000 Indians live on these reservations, and about another 150,000 outside them. Although the size and quality of their reservations vary, they all have one thing in common—abject poverty. They suffer from housing so bad that one estimate has suggested that 90 per cent of all Indians live in nothing better than tin-roofed shacks, poor quality mud huts, rough shelters, and old cars. About 60 per cent of them have no water supply nearby, many people having to walk over a mile to fetch it. Although the Indians lived with these hardships before the enforcement of

the reservations they were a part of their culture. Now, with their culture changing under the influence of urban man, they still have to suffer these hardships, but enjoy neither the benefits of modern civilization nor the freedom of their original way of life.

Unemployment among Indians is at least 10 times higher than among other Americans, while their average wage is less than a quarter of the national average. Similarly, the average age of death for Indians is 43, compared with 68 for white Americans. A great many diseases are suffered much more by the Indians than by the rest of the population. For example, dysentery is 40 times more frequent, influenza twice as frequent. An Indian baby is less likely to reach the age of one than are other Americans to reach the age of 40.

Perhaps, however, the most humiliating aspect of the plight of the Amerindians in the United States is the educational system that has been imposed upon them. Most children are removed from their homes and sent to barracklike board-

With little or no thought for their community requirements, the Eskimos are presented with dull lines of concrete huts.

ing schools. Not only do these schools alienate the children and partially isolate them from their culture, they also produce a suicide rate twice the national average for that age group. It is not uncommon for children as young as eight years to commit suicide.

Given their appalling conditions it is surprising that the Indians remain on their reservations. But they do, and what is more they have vigorously resisted any attempt to remove them or to reduce the reservations still further. For although the reservations are on the whole grossly inadequate—in terms of size and quality of land—they are all that the Indians have, the symbol of their culture, the home of their memories.

These reservations are the results of treaties between the U.S. Government and the Amerindian tribes. About a third were peace treaties, and the remainder were land cessions. In other words, the U.S. Government permanently guaranteed the Indians their reservation land in return for generally much larger areas of land ceded by the Indians. In all but a very few cases,

the guarantees were for ever—for "as long as the rivers run and the grass grows"—and were promises that the Indians could occupy their reservations absolutely free of all interference by anybody. If the reservations were so small that the Indians could not hunt in them, then they were given goods and often a small annual grant in compensation. But much the most important aspect of these treaties was that they confirmed the principle of Indian sovereignty: in each case the U.S. Government dealt with an independent nation. Unfortunately, while it could not avoid confirming this principle, the U.S.A. in all other respects treated the Indians as racial and cultural inferiors. So great has been the white Americans contempt for their hosts, that they have consistently violated their treaties. Treaty land has been compulsorily purchased and annexed, even though under international law the treaties are valid. The Indians have

121

never been accorded their rights as citizens of sovereign nations, nor have they been offered full compensatory rights as citizens of the U.S.A. Worse still, the land treaties were interpreted very differently by the Indians and by the Whites. As with many of the other representatives of natural man, only a few of the Indian tribes had any concept of the ownership of land. Most knew only of the right to use the land and enjoy the fruits of it. As a result, they ceded treaty rights very willingly, assuming that the Europeans wanted to use the land for no longer than a few seasons, and quite unaware that they intended to settle permanently.

By the 1880s, the United States had completed their conquest of the Indians, all of whom were by then confined to their reservations. But the shock of defeat and of the loss of so much land was followed by the still greater humiliation of a campaign to "civilize" them. Proud and independent hunters were forced to turn to farming, which in any case they were obliged to do since they no longer had enough land to support the food-collecting way of life. But the white Americans went further: they made it clear that they regarded hunting as a slothful and degrading activity, no substitute for the true and dignified labor of agriculture. Missionaries were given the run of the reservations and allowed to do what they liked in their task of converting the Indians. They appeared to accept it as their function to convert the Indians as much to the white American way of life as to Christianity. They outlawed Indian religions, rituals, and gatherings, not so much because they were pagan but merely because they were Indian. Despite overwhelming odds, however, many tribes managed to retain their councils and their basic social structure.

The Indians had also managed to retain a total of 139 million acres of land west of the Mississippi River, and were gradually becoming reconciled to a farming way of life. Then in 1887 the General Allotment Act was passed, which allowed the President to give tribal land to individual Indians. The theory was that the Indians should learn to farm like white men, individually and not communally, and that the communal land ownership of the Indians was hindering their progress toward civilization. In practice, how-

Navaho Indians sell beads on their reservation in the Little Colorado River Gorge, near the Grand Canyon.

In Canada, the arrival of the European gave the Indian the opportunity to sell furs at the cost of reducing game.

An Indian resets his snare after retrieving a hare. Hares provide an important and regular source of food for trappers.

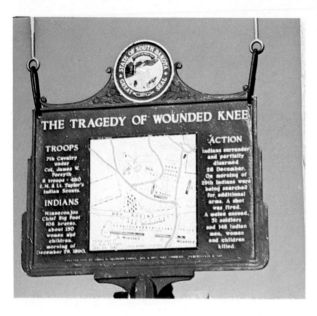

Conflict still mars relationships between Indian and white American. The plaque above commemorates the tragedy of Wounded Knee in 1890, where 146 Minneconjou Indians, including unarmed women and children, were killed by U.S. cavalry and the shellfire from a Hotchkiss cannon.

In 1971 members of the sun dance cult, an Indian revival religion, came into conflict with tribal authorities who objected to their allegedly disruptive effect. Below, an Indian member of the cult in ritual dress taking part in a sun dance.

The conflict known as the Second Battle of Wounded Knee in 1973 deteriorated into an armed confrontation between Indians and white authority. Above: dancers gather around the sacred sun dance pole. In the background is the occupied church.

ever, it was a means of eroding the reservations. Once individual Indians owned the land one of the most important ways of holding the tribe together disappeared. But most of the Indians did not take up the offer, and in many cases it was assumed that they therefore did not want the land, and white Americans were allowed to settle on it. In this way over 100 reservations, largely in the Great Lakes, Pacific Coast, and Plains regions, disappeared. The loss of land did not end there. The plots the Indians were allowed to buy were too small to support a family, and were often re-sold to Whites. Between 1887 and 1933, 90,000 Indians were made homeless, and 91 million acres of their land were lost, two-thirds of the little they were allowed after conquest. This is

the prime cause of much Indian poverty today.

In 1934, the situation was partially alleviated by the Indian Reorganization Act, which recognized the Indians' acute economic and cultural need for land. An annual grant of $2 million was allocated for the purchase of land, and during the next 10 years 50 million acres were bought for the tribes, and much land was improved by intelligent conservation measures. The architect of the Act was John Collier, the only Commissioner of Indian Affairs with a true appreciation of Indian needs. He alone realized the absolute necessity for maintaining the tribal community if the Indians were not to collapse into a demoralized third-class citizenry.

Unfortunately, his successors have not been so enlightened, and since the Second World War the preoccupation of the U.S. Government has been to detribalize the Indians as quickly as possible, whether they like it or not. This was the aim of the 1953 termination bill, which, under the guise of terminating what was described as a humiliat-

A teepee was set up at Wounded Knee as a neutral negotiating place between the Indians and Federal officials.

ingly paternalistic relationship between the Government and the tribes, in fact allowed the Government to arbitrarily end Indian title to land without reference to the people affected. Fortunately, the Indians and their friends have managed in most cases to resist the bill, but not before a number of tribes have been effectively eliminated by it. The Klamath tribe of Oregon, for example, suddenly found itself being told that unless it gave up its land without fuss it would not be entitled to compensation. The result was that in one stroke it lost its treaty rights, which although more honored in the breach, are still a vital legal weapon. In addition, the tribes simply ceased to exist as a distinct entity. Then, as the land was no longer owned by the tribe but by individuals, it ceased to be tax exempt. The timber stands were sold and the proceeds distributed among the members of the tribe, each one receiving about

$43,000. None of them were used to a cash economy, let alone to handling so much money, and of course they spent it as fast as they could. Finally, the Klamath people were easy prey to white people who wanted their land and persuaded them to sell it cheaply.

The termination bill is barbaric for two main reasons. First, it strikes at the root of Indian dignity, removing their security without making any real attempt to help them adjust to a workable alternative. And secondly, it violates not just the Indians' treaty rights and the Federal guarantees that such rights would always be protected, but also the promises by treaty that the

Below: Indians occupied the Bureau of Indian Affairs in November 1972. The building was to them a symbol of 100 years of bureaucratic oppression. They even prepared Molotov cocktails in case police stormed the building (above).

Above: Dennis Banks, director of the American Indian Movement, a militant and activist organization that campaigns for Indian rights, speaking outside the Bureau of Indian Affairs.

Indians would have permanent and inalienable title to their lands.

The Indians of North America have rarely been treated honorably by their European conquerors. They have been often deceived, slaughtered, and humiliated. It might be assumed that the Americans of today would be anxious to make amends for the inhuman behavior of some of their forefathers. Sadly, this seems far from the case.

The Indians of the United States, however,

have a distinct advantage over the Indians of Brazil and the other countries of tropical South America. For while those of the North are now experienced in the ways of the white man and are learning to fight with him on his own terms, their brothers in the South have no meeting points with the dominant culture save those of disease and the gun.

Out of the estimated 1 to 5 million Amerindians who lived in Brazil, only about 75,000 are left. Some of them have been reduced to the squalor of the shanty towns, while others belong to virtually isolated tribes. These latter still hunt, fish, and garden as they have done for thousands of years. They are still truly natural men, but they are highly vulnerable to the depredations of the city men.

Brazil's Indians have been decimated by disease and by violence. They have no resistance to diseases such as measles, smallpox, tuberculosis, and the common cold, which have spread like wildfire with devastating effect. Those who have managed to survive such diseases have often fallen prey to the greed of the white man. The rest have been utterly demoralized, either directly by missionaries who have censured their customs, or indirectly by the invading culture. The technological gimmickry of our way of life, while it

does not offer an appealing substitute for their own culture, quite often undermines the Indians' faith in it. To be deprived of faith in all that you value can be as devastating as being deprived of the means of subsistence.

There have been attempts to try and do something about the Amerindians' plight. In 1910, the great Candido Rondon inspired and helped to found Brazil's Indian Protection Service (SPI). Under him the Service helped to alleviate much of the suffering and to prevent further hardship. It helped secure tribal lands and it provided some sort of medical and educational assistance. It was deliberately neutral about religion, and stood for the honoring and respect of the tribal way of life. Thanks to the early work of the SPI, many tribes survived that would otherwise have disintegrated.

Unfortunately, the SPI soon became subject to political pressure. In the 1930s, Rondon quarreled with President Vargas, and the SPI was almost disbanded and lost its financial support. A country whose Constitution guarantees the Indians' possession of their lands thereafter found itself unable to uphold that guarantee for want of a strong enough protection service. With its ludicrously slender budget, the SPI found itself forced to employ men unfitted to the task. Often it lacked enough money for elementary medical assistance, let alone for legal aid in land disputes.

Such legal aid became decreasingly available as it grew increasingly necessary. Ambiguous phrasing in the Brazilian Constitution made it possible for states to take control of Indian lands from the Federal Government, thereby making the constitutional protection of those lands worthless. Many Indians were forced to flee their homes and local politicians curried votes by persuading their electorate that Indian land was theirs for the taking. Occasionally such people were taken to court, but usually such actions came to nothing.

The years following World War II witnessed a succession of scandals. In the 1940s and 1950s, the great Xavante tribe was reduced to a handful of despised groups, squatting at mission stations or on the edges of the cattle ranches that took over their territory. The Cayapo were destroyed by disease—transmitted by expeditions sent out to save them from rubber tappers who would otherwise have massacred them. The remnants of a number of other tribes decimated by disease were either slaughtered or driven off their land. In 1967, the Brazilian Government ordered an enquiry into the plight of the Amerindians. The result was the Figueiredo Report, which demonstrated that many of the SPI's 800 employees were corrupt, and exposed a history of cruelty. The SPI was subsequently abolished and replaced by a new organization called the National Indian Foundation, or FUNAI. Unfortunately, up to now FUNAI seems to have been unable to protect the Indians from alien diseases and from land-

Below: the new Amerindians of the tropics. Integration and assimilation generally means a collapse into poverty.

Right: the trans-Amazonian highway slices through the forests of Brazil, endangering the habitat of the Indians.

grabbers, still their two greatest scourges.

This is not to say that the Amerindians lack helpers. Their two greatest ones came from the SPI itself. They are the Villas-Boas brothers, Orlando and Claudio. In the late 1940s, they joined an expedition to the upper Xingu River. They stayed behind to form the Xingu National Park. In this area, the indigenous people have been able to live as they wish, free from outside interference. And into it, the Villas-Boas brothers have brought other tribes—the ones threatened by development or colonization. These peoples are not kept as museum pieces, but are free to live as they wish, being provided with technical and other education as they require it. Most, however, have chosen to continue their traditional way of life—living proof that there are other ways of helping the Indians besides stealing their lands and forcibly assimilating them. The Xingu National Park has been under more or less constant pressure, and the Villas-Boas brothers have had to fight many battles to stop encroachments on the Park and even prevent its total abolition. They were remarkably successful, until in 1971 a presidential decree removed a third of the Park containing the beautiful forest and river lands to which the Indians are adapted, giving them in exchange open bushland—land which is quite unsuitable.

Discouraged by this inexplicable blow, the Villas-Boas Brothers have announced their intention of giving up. They and the handful of dedicated men and women like them who battle on within FUNAI and similar organizations need as much help as they can get, from whatever quarter. So do the Amerindians and the other tribal minorities like them scattered across the tropical regions of the world. One of the few organizations formed specifically to meet this need is the London-based Survival International.

Left: the two men who founded the Xingu National Park in Brazil, Claudio (left) and Orlando Villas-Boas. Below: the Villas-Boas brothers, pioneers of the struggle to save the Amerindians, pictured with some of the Indians they have befriended.

An airstrip in the forest, hacked out by the Villas-Boas team so that a tribe could be persuaded into the Xingu National Park before its lands were destroyed by industrialization.

A young Amerindian using an outboard motor. The Indians in the Xingu Park are free to live their traditional way of life, adopt a modern one, or choose a compromise, as they wish.

In 1967, a handful of concerned individuals got together to form an Amerindian Protection Trust. When news of the Figueiredo Report was published, they joined with others to form the Primitive Peoples Fund, a charity dedicated to helping tribal minorities not just in South America but all over the world. Later still, the trust changed its name to Survival International, though its objects remain unchanged: to secure the traditional land rights of tribal minorities, to provide them with legal and medical assistance where necessary, and to help them either to preserve their way of life or to adapt to modern ways according to their choice. Survival International has sent out survey expeditions to Brazil and Indonesia to assess the position and needs of tribal minorities in both countries. It compiles an up-to-date dossier on tribal minorities through-

The Villas-Boas' plane brings the brothers and their team to all the tribes in the Xingu Park, who warmly welcome them.

out the world. And it provides as much aid as funds allow.

Bodies such as Survival International play a vital role in helping peoples so unused to the ways of the industrial world that they are unable to help themselves. But peoples such as the Eskimos, the Australian Aborigines, and the North American Indians, have begun to help themselves. Former generations of these peoples remained bewildered by their fate and by the technological ingenuity and sophisticated double-talk of the white man. But their children have learned the ways of the dominant culture, evaluated them, and elected to lead their own way of life. They have chosen the weapons of white society to fight for a synthesis of what they judge to be the best of traditional customs and the best of modern ones.

As might be expected, this development is most marked in the United States. There are a number of political and cultural groups among the Indians of the U.S.A., whose main object is the continued survival of their people as living tribes. One of the most interesting and encouraging developments is the adaptation of industrial techniques to the traditional way of life by some of the tribes.

The most famous example is that of the Yankton Sioux in South Dakota. The Yankton are descendants of proud hunters, and they wanted to benefit from modern technology without suffering the kinds of social and emotional destruction that is associated with full

133

Mining is often presented as an opportunity for wealth, but for the North American Indians, who lack both the skills and the inclination to mine, it means only the ruin of land.

indeed have promise and recommending a grant of $115,000 in order that the existing makeshift factory could be replaced. His plans included landscaping, a multilane highway, all the trappings of a modern industrial estate.

This was exactly the sort of situation that the Indians most disliked. All they wanted, their spokesman said, was $8000 so that they could carry on with their own version of progress and not somebody else's. He had to go back to his people empty-handed. The Bureau of Indian Affairs had its own ideas about development and thought the Yanktons' rather absurd.

Fortunately, the Yanktons got their money from the Episcopal Church of Boston. Today, their factory is a model of its kind. There are no labor disputes and there is no time clock. Each man can come and go as he pleases. He can work conventional hours and take conventional holidays, or he can work nonstop for a week and take a whole month off. He gets paid a basic minimum, and then anything above that depends on how much work he says he has done. Because the Sioux are still capable of living a true community life, they trust each other and behave responsibly toward each other. Accordingly, they enjoy more freedom than we do, and a more rewarding working life.

Natural man's relationships with urban man have entered a new era. Those peoples who are still leading relatively traditional lives are close to being entirely eliminated. They require vigorous protection by all nations if they are to survive at all, and slowly, groups are being formed all over the world to press for such protection and to help provide the means for it. Those other peoples who suffered the traumas of contact with urban man some years ago have begun to learn not to rely on the parsimonious charity of the white man. They are learning, too, not to look up to the dominant culture, but to appreciate its many defects as well as its virtues. They have begun the arduous struggle for the right and the opportunity to lead their own lives as they wish, to fashion anew a culture that is not buried in the past—a modern one that is peculiarly their own.

Apart from humanitarian reasons and from the fact that we can discover many curious items of behavior from him, is there any point in trying to save natural man? Is there anything of real value that we can learn from him? The answer is yes. We can classify the sorts of information we can

industrialization. They began by converting their community hall into an electronic components factory. Soon they were providing jobs for 40 of their men and were much respected by the companies they supplied for their strict adherence to delivery dates.

In time they decided they would like to expand, not because they had fallen in love with profits or wanted to consolidate their position, nor for any other business motive. It was simply that they were anxious to help their brothers, the Santee Sioux, who lived on the other side of the Missouri River. With a larger plant, they could provide jobs for 50 of the Santee men during the lean winter months.

They needed $8000 for new tools, so they sent a spokesman to the Bureau of Indian Affairs in Washington to ask for the money. The Commissioner was impressed and sent one of his specialists to find out if the factory was as efficient as it sounded. The specialist returned saying it did

Some attempt is being made to train Aborigines for life among the alien people and the alien culture that surround them. Many Aborigines, however, would simply prefer to return to their traditional land and way of life.

A lumberjack fells a tree in the heart of equatorial Africa. Habitats such as this forest should be maintained in their entirety for the benefit of the peoples that inhabit them, to conserve the plant gene pools, and for undiscovered data they may contain.

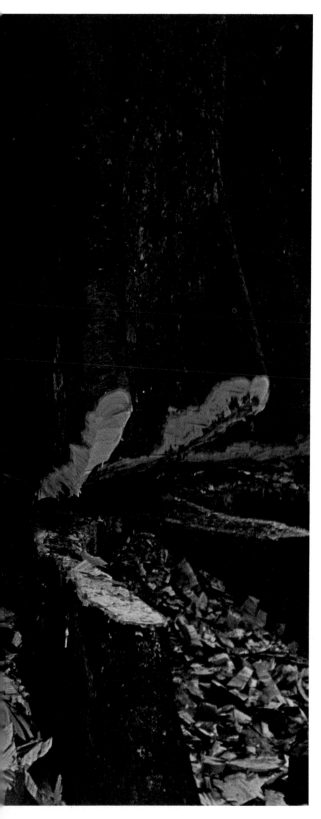

discover from natural man into two categories: direct and indirect. In the direct category comes his considerable knowledge of the natural world—his knowledge of plants and animals. In the indirect one, come the basic principles we can derive from a study of his social behavior and institutions.

All of today's surviving hunter-gatherer and hunter-gardener groups live in relatively undisturbed environments. These are also the world's most important sources of genetic diversity, of the plants and animals that form the gene pools of many of the foodstuffs and drugs on which we depend. The conservation of such genetic diversity is essential if the world is to continue feeding itself. This is because pests and diseases evolve new varieties faster than domestic plants evolve resistance to them. Accordingly, we have to hybridize new plant varieties in order to maintain and improve yields. We might take one variety of wheat noted for its high protein content and hybridize it with one noted for its resistance to fungal disease, for example. This work depends on the conservation of all the original varieties.

In addition, there are probably a great many plants with still undiscovered nutritional, medicinal, and mechanical properties. If the areas in which they live are destroyed, we shall never be able to use them and a priceless asset will have been lost. For these reasons, the United Nations Conference on the Human Environment, held at Stockholm in June 1972, strongly recommended that large tracts of forest, bushland, and grassland, be conserved as evolving plant gene pools. These habitats can only be conserved if they are maintained in their entirety, that is, complete with the peoples that inhabit them.

But having conserved these areas, what then? There is, of course, nothing wrong with leaving well enough alone; but it is of the utmost importance that we learn as quickly as possible what they contain. The tribes of hunter-gatherers and hunter-gardeners who live in them, have done so for thousands of generations. They have learned a great deal about the properties of plants there, and much about the animals. It is only sensible to find out what they know, before we do anything else. Unfortunately, this is not as simple as it sounds. It is not a question of going into the jungle with mobile laboratories, batteries of cameras and tape recorders, and squads of scientists skilled in interviewing techniques.

This is a recipe for getting false information very fast or no information at all. What are needed are ethnobotanists and ethnozoologists—men and women who know something of plants and animals, but more importantly are prepared to live with a tribe, without interrogating its members. Instead they should observe them closely, note exactly every use to which plants and animals are put, and simply seek the people's help in identifying them.

The study of natural man's social behavior and institutions is no less important and requires even more specialized techniques. First of all a thorough anthropological understanding of the tribe is necessary. In addition, experts are needed in whatever aspect is considered to be of prime importance, health, nutrition, and so on. The modern industrial world is troubled by many ills that may not necessarily be inevitable. They are probably products of our particular culture, rather than innately human. We can only find out whether or not we are naturally violent, greedy, or power-mad through a study of natural man. Similarly, we can learn from him a variety of ways of ensuring social harmony, of curing psychological disorders, and so on. This does not mean that we should adopt the Bushmen's trance dance or the institution of the shaman, or in any other way attempt to duplicate hunter-gatherer social organization. All it means is that by studying basic principles of such social organization, we can find out whether or not ours is constructed along the right lines, and if not, what reforms might be possible.

By the same token we can answer many difficult questions about health and what is the best type of diet through a study of hunter-gatherer health and nutrition. Again this does not mean to say that we should adopt identical menus to those of the Eskimos, or of the Andaman Islanders. It does mean that we might discover a vital nutritional principle that has so far evaded us or confirm others that at the moment are in dispute.

Both the industrial and the nonindustrial countries of the world face an increasing number of seemingly insoluble social and economic problems. Their solution requires courage and imagination, but imagination must not be entirely unfettered. It has to be restricted to what is humanly possible. The study of natural man, besides demonstrating the wonderful diversity of mankind, is exactly that—the study of the humanly possible.

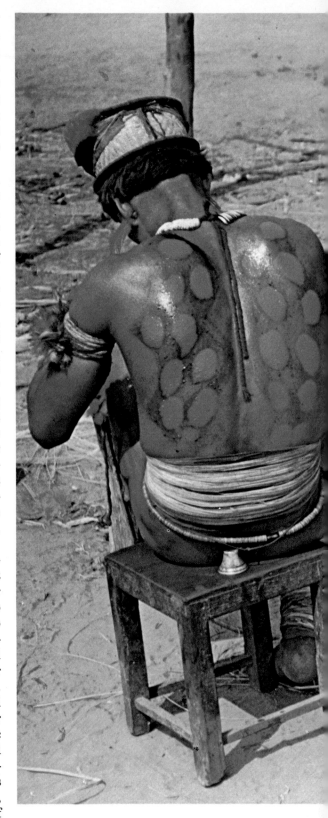

Kamayura Indians with their pets in the Xingu National Park. This is the only place in Brazil where the Indians can live as they wish. In spite of all their efforts the park is being dismembered, and the Villas-Boas brothers have resigned in despair.

Index

Page numbers in *italics* refer to captions to illustrations.

Abortifacients, plants used as, 70, 74

abortion, control of population by, 34, 74, 76

adaptation: biological and cultural, 13; optimum level of, 34–5

addax antelope, 57

adolescence, 114–17

agriculture: development of, *34*, 35, 36; percentage of mankind occupied in, 29; slash-and-burn, or swidden, *48*, 49, *49*, 50, *50–1*

Ainu people (Japan), fishing by, 43

Aleuts, anatomical knowledge possessed by, 66

American Indian Movement, *126*

Amerindian Protection Trust, 132

Amerindians: fishing by, 40; food plants of, 51, 67–8, *66–7*; institution of chiefs among, 84, *84–5*; present plight of, 118, *119*; *see also individual peoples and areas*

Andaman Islanders: honey-gathering by, 68; puberty rites among, 114, 117

animals: domestication of, 35, 36; gene pools of, 137; natural man's knowledge of, 23, 62, 64, 137; totemic, 95

arrow poisons, *20*, 68, *98*

Australian Aborigines, *9*, *32–3*, *60–1*; children of, *112–13*; food gathering by, 45, *45–6*, 46; ritualization of violence by, 78, *78*, *79*; totems of, 60–1, *61*, 95, *95*; *see also individual tribes*

Australopithecus, fossil manlike ape, 10, *12*

auwa, sacred place of Australian clan, 60, 61

Banks, Dennis, director of American Indian Movement, *126*

Bantu, and Bushmen, *16*, *32*

Barama River Caribs (Guyana), and spirits of trees, 60

baskets and bags, 70

beehives, of Majangir, 104

behavior patterns, development of new, 13

Bella Coola people (Northwest America), 43

blood of cattle, as food, 52

blowpipe, *38*

boat-building, *104–5*; model, *113*

Bomagai-Angoiang people (New Guinea); gardens of, 99; pigs of, 53, 100; prestige among, 104

Botswana, Bushmen in, 16

bows and arrows: for fishing, *42*, for hunting, 20, 64; learning to use, 114, *114*

brain, of apes and man, *8*, *11*, 13

Brazil, Amerindians of, *32*, *42*, *43*, *46*; remains of population of, 127; struggle to save, 127–33

buffalo (bison), hunting of by Amerindians, 38

buffalo (African) hunting of: by Majangir, 36; by Pygmies, *36–7*

Bunyoro people (Uganda), Chief Winyi IV of, *86*, *87*

Bureau of Indian Affairs, U.S.A.: building of, occupied by Indians (*1973*), *126*; Sioux and, 134

Bushmen, 16, *17*, *18*, *19*, *20*, *21*, *22*, *23*, *32*; children of, 110, 111; food supply of, 16, 18–21, 23; have no shamans, 90; hunting by, *36–7*; hunting gestures of, *64*, *65*; personal properties of, *98*; social life of, *23–8*; *see also Dobe !Kung, G/wi, !Kung, and Nyae Nyae !Kung Bushmen*

Canada, fur-hunting in, *123*

cancer, almost absent from Solomon Islanders, 74

cannibalism, 78

caribou: hunting of, by Eskimos, 36

cattle, in Africa, 51, 52, *53*

Cayapo people (Brazil), destroyed by disease, 128

chiefs: African, *86–7*, Amerindian, 84, *84–5*, 86, 87

child-rearing, 108–14

Chimbu people (New Guinea), war game of, *82*

Chimpanzee, brain of, *11*

Chippewa Indians (Minnesota), harvesting of wild rice by, 44, *44*, 45

clams, preserving of, 43

clans: matrilineal, patrilineal, and geographical, 95; totems of, 60, 95

cocaine, 68, *68*, *69*

Collier, John, Commissioner of Indian Affairs, U.S.A., 125

Colorado people (Ecuador), *69*

Comanche people (North America), shamans of, 92, 95

communities: of Bushmen, 18; dealing with tensions in, 78, 80–1; democracy in, 84, 89; splitting and recombination of, 26, 81

containers, gourds as, 70

contraception: control of population by, 34, 74, 76; plants used for, 70, 74

co-operation: in clearing forest, 51; in hunting, 36, 38

Corroboree ceremony, *101*

crocodiles, Amerindian knowledge of, 64

Cro-Magnon man, 13

Cubeo people (Colombia): cultivators, 71; communal long-houses of, 81; headmen and building of long-houses by, 86–7, *88–9*, 89

curare, 68

Damon, Dr Albert, on health of Solomon Islanders, 73

dances: emu-mimicking, of Australian Aborigines, *64*; sundance cult, U.S.A., *124*; trance of medicine, of Bushmen, 26, *26–7*, 28

democracy, of hunter-gatherer societies, 84, 89

derris insecticide, 40, 68

detribalization, of Indians by U.S. Government, 125

diseases: epidemic, a recent aberration? 30; introduced to nonimmune populations, 74, 76, 127, 128; of Indians in U.S.A., 120; life of natural man relatively free from, 24, 73

divorce, 25, 108

Dobe !Kung Bushmen, 16, 97

dogs, in fishing by Ainu, 43

Dorobo people (Kenya), attitude of, to animals, 58

dreaming, centered around totems, 95

drugs, possible development of new, 40

Dryopithecus, fossil ape, 10

duiker, hunted by Bushmen, *20*

Dyak (Borneo), drying meat, *97*

Education: of Indians in U.S.A., 120–1; of natural man, by involvement, 111–14
elephants, hunting of, by Pygmies, 38
Eripagtsa women (Brazil): gather honey, 46; make basket, 71
Eskimos, 14–15, 32, 89; behavior of, toward animals killed, 57; complete utilization of animals by, 64, 66; housing supplied for, 121; hunting by, 36, 38, 56, 57; infanticide among, 74; knowledge of animals by, 64; knowledge of sea ice by, 62
Ethnobotanists and ethnozoologists, need for, 138
evolution: of man, 8, 10; rate of, 13
eyes of primates, position of, 8

Factory, fitting into community life of Sioux, 133–4
family, 105–8
Figueiredo Report, on plight of Indians in Brazil, 128, 132
fishing, 36, 38, 40; areas depending on, 43; by poisons, 40, 68; techniques of, 40, 40–1, 42, 43, 43; by urban man, 38
food gathering: areas depending on, 43; by urban man, 44; by women (Australian Aborigine), 45; (Bushmen) 20, 22
food plants: Amerindians' list of, 50, 64, 66, 66–7; cultivation of mixtures of, 49; domestication of, 35, 51, 71
forests: attitude of natural man toward, 57–8; need to preserve, 136, 137; origin of man in, 10, 13
Fulani (West Africa), herdsmen, 52

General Allotment Act, U.S.A. (1887), 122
generosity, as a virtue, 24; prestige from, 84, 100, 103, 104
giraffe, bowl made from kneecap of, 20
glacier, Mount Kenya, 30–1
grasshoppers, as food, 38
green peppers, juice of, 69
Guyana, Amerindians of, 58
G/wi Bushmen. and scorpions, 58

Haiari fish poison, 68
hallucinogens, from plants, 70 90, 92, 92
hammocks, of Amerindians, 99, 110
Hanunoo people (Philippines), swidden cultivators, 49
harpoons, 38
Havasu Canyon, Arizona, 76–7
Havasupai people (Arizona), 76
health, of natural man, 73, 138
heart disease, almost absent from Solomon Islanders, 73
herdsmen, nomadic, 52
hides, uses for, 23, 38, 66
hoarding, considered antisocial, 23, 99
Hobbes, Thomas, 29
Homo erectus, 11
Homo sapiens neanderthalensis, 10, 12
Homo sapiens sapiens, 12
honey, gathering of, 46, 47, 66, 68
honey wine, 48, 104
Hong Kong shanty town, 28–9
hospital, effect of, on Havasupai population, 76
housing: of Bushmen, 18–19; of Eskimos in Canada, 121; of Indians in U.S.A., 118, 119 120; of Pygmies, 28
Humboldt, F.H.A. von, 62
hunter-gatherers, percentage of mankind included in, 30
hunting: by Bushmen, 18–20, 20, 21; status acquired by skill in, 103; techniques of, 36, 38; by urban man, 36
Hupa people (California), identify child with spruce tree, 56
husbands, hunting ability of, 26, 108

Ice Age: disruption of relation between man and nature by, 30, 35; map showing extent of ice cap in, 32–3
Indian Protection Service, Brazil (SPI), 128, 131
Indian Reorganization Act, U.S.A. (1934), 125
Industrial Revolution, 34
infant mortality, among Bushmen, 24
infanticide, control of population by, 34, 74

insects, repellent for, 69
Israel, series of human bones found in, 13

Jalé people (New Guinea): boys of, 115; men's houses of, 117; warriors of, 80, 81
jimson weed, hallucinogenic, 90
jojonghe plant, as protection against bees, 68

Kalahari Desert, 16
Kalahari Park, 16
Kalapolo Indian (Brazil), 42
Kamayura Indians (Brazil), 116, 138–9; bark canoes of, 70–1; flute players of, 92
Karaja, scarification of body by, 92
Karam people (New Guinea), on comparison of women and pigs, 53
Karamojong (Uganda), herdsmen, 52
karosses, garments of Bushman women, 20
kinship structures, 105, 108
Klamath tribe (Oregon), lose their land, 125–6
Kraho people (Brazil), shaman of, 92
Kuikuru people (South America), cultivation of manioc by, 50
!Kung Bushmen, 20, 23, 23, 24, 26, 72; children of, 111; have a horror of fighting, 78
Kwaio people (Solomon Islands), health of, 73

Lactation for long periods, 108; in population control, 72
land: communal ownership of, by Indians in U.S.A., 122; ownership of cleared, 99, 100
Lapps, herdsmen, 52, 52–3
laughter, propensity for, as Bushmen virtue, 24
leadership, in natural man communities, 84–90
Leakey, Richard, and skull of manlike ape, 10, 10, 11, 12, 30
Lesu people (New Ireland): aborti-

facient and contraceptive plants known by, 68, 70; children among, 110; ownership of cleared land among, 99
long-houses, of Cubeo people, 86–7, *88–9*

Maize (Indian corn), staple crop in North and Central America, 50–1, 67
Majangir people (Ethiopia): crafts of, 70; drinking parties of, 82; honey-gathering by, 47–8; hunting by, 38; prestige among, 104; smoking of meat by, 98; use of hides by, 66
Makuna people (Colombia), boat-makers of, *104–5*
manioc: cultivation of, 50; staple crop in Africa and South America, 51, 67
marriage, 25–6, 108
Masai people (East Africa), herds-men, 52, *53*
Mbuti Pygmies (Zaire), *28*; betrothal festival of, 108; and the forest, 58; hunting by, 38
meat: areas depending on, 43; in diet, 23, 36; drying of, *25, 96, 97*; sharing of, 23, *24–5, 97*; smoking of, 97; stored in ice, 36
medicinal plants, 58, 68, 70
medicine, preventive, 35
Melanesia, pigs, in, 52
melons, gathered by Bushmen women, 20, *22*
milk, as food, 52
millet, staple crop in African grasslands, 51
missionaries, among Amerindians: in Brazil, 127; in U.S.A., 122
Mohawks, graveyard of, 120
Mongongo (mangetti) nut, 16, 67
Mundjutj fruit, Arnhem Land, 46

Napore tribe (Uganda), hunting by, *39*
Nasioi people (Solomon Islands), health of, 73
National Indian Foundation, Brazil (FUNAI), 128, 131
nature: natural man's knowledge of, 60–70; natural man's re-lation with, 53, 56–60; relation

with, emphasized by totemism, 95
Navaho people (North America): reservation of, 120, *122*; shamans of, *90–1*
Neanderthal man, 10, 13
Neel, J. V., on health of Xavante and Yanomamo peoples, 73
Nelson, Richard, anthropologist, 62
Nemadi people (Mauritania), and addax, 57
Netsilik Eskimo, dyadic partner-ships among, 89
neurotic characters, of some shamans, 92
New Guinea: bows and arrows in, *114–15*; headdress of warriors in, *102–3*; pigs in, 52; *see also individual peoples*
New Hebrides, abortifacient and contraceptive plants known in, 68
nomads, possessions of, 24
nonviolence, as Bushman virtue, 24
Nootka people (Northwest America), 43
Nyae Nyae !Kung Bushmen, sharing of meat by, *24–5, 97*

Oil, from fish, 43
Ojibwa people (Minnesota), harvesting of wild rice by, 44, *44*, 45
old people: care of, 108; proportion of, in Bushman population, 24
Omaha people (North America), and medicinal plants, 58
orangutans, *8–9*
ostriches, Bushmen pretend to hunt, *65*
overcrowding, diseases of, 35

Paints and dyes, exchanges in-volving (Australia), 100
Panare people (Venezuela), in forest camp, *58–9*
Parapithecus, fossil ape, 10
parasitic worms, in Bushmen compared with other rural African populations, 73
peyote, hallucinogenic, 90
pigs in New Guinea, 52, 99–100

Pinatubo Negritos (Philippines), plant knowledge of, 71
Pitjantjatjara people (Australia), children of, *114–15*
plants: domestication of, 35, 51, 71; gathering of, *see* food gather-ing; gene pools of, 70, 137; hallucinogenic, 70, 90, 92, *92*; medicinal, 58, 66, 68; natural man's knowledge of, 23, 64, 68, 70, 137; *see also* food plants
poisons: on arrows, *20*, 68, *98*; on darts, *38*; for fish, 40, 68
polygamy, among Tiwi (Australia), 46–7
population, cultural control of growth of, 34–6, 71, 73–4, 76
potatoes, staple crop in Andes, 51, 67
poverty, recent aberration? 30
preservation of food: of fish by drying and smoking, 43; of meat by drying, *96, 97*, freezing, 36, and smoking, 98
primates, 8
Primitive People's Fund, 132
Proconsul, fossil chimpanzee, 10
property, attitudes toward, 24, 97–100
protein, intake of, by Bushmen, 16
psilocybe mushrooms, hallucino-genic, 90
puberty rites, 108, 114, 117
Pygmies (Zaire forest), *14, 28, 32, 33, 109*; hunting by, *36–7*, 38; *see also* Mbuti Pygmies

Quinine, 66

Reciprocity, principle of, 99, 100
reindeer, of Lapps, 52, *52–3*
religion of natural man, 90–5
reservations, for Indians in U.S.A., 120–6
rice: in Philippines, (grown dry), 49, (grown in paddies), *34*; staple crop in Southeast Asia, 51; wild, 44, *44, 45*, 45
rifles, of Eskimos, *56*
rock paintings: of fish totem, *61*; of Saharan game, 35
role, prestige from harmonious fulfillment of, 102–3
Rondon, Candido, founder of SPI,

Brazil, 128
ropes, from vines, 70

S ahara Desert, rock painting of game in, *35*
Sanpoil tribe (Northwest America), Salmon Chief appointed by, 40, 97
Santee Sioux, 134
seaweed, as food, 44
sex totems, 95
shamans (medicine men), 90–5
sharing, ethic of, 23–4, *24–5*, 84, 99
sheep, ranching of (Australia), *34–5*
shellfish, gathering of, *46–7*
Shoshone people (North America), hunting by, 38
Sioux people (North America), *32*, 133–4
Siriono people (Bolivia), 111
snakes, Dorobo attitude to, 58
social organization of natural man, study of, 138
Solomon Islands: bachelors' houses in, *73*; health in, 73
sorghum, staple crop in African grasslands, 51
spears, 38, 40
spirit quests, by Amerindian boys, 56
Springhaas, hunted by, Bushmen, *21*
standard of living, of hunter-gatherers, 28–9
status, 100, 102–4
steam baths, and fertility of Havasupai men, 76
stock-raising, development of, *34–5*, 36
stone axes, exchanges involving (Australia), 100
sugar, effects of eating excess of, 13
suicide, among Indian children in U.S.A., 121
Survival International, 131–2
sweet potatoes, cultivation of (New Guinea), *100*
swidden (slash-and-burn) agriculture, *48*, 49, *49*, 50, *50–1*, 51

T apirupe people (Brazil), regula-

ted numbers of, 74, 76
tarsiers, in ancestry of man, 10
Tasaday people (Philippines), makers of stone tools, 74, *75*, *106–7*
teeth: of primates, 8; sugar and, 13
Tenetehara people (Brazil), expansionist, 74
Tepoztlan (Mexico), swidden agriculture of, 50
termination bill, U.S.A. (1953), 125, 126
theft, almost unknown to natural man, 98–9
Tiwi people (Australia): duels and group disputes among, 82–3; polygamy among, 46
Tlingit people (Northwest America), 43
tobacco, 58, 68
Tokelau people (Polynesia), identify child with trees, 56
totem poles, Alaska, *94*
totems, of Australian Aborigines, 60, 61, *61*, 95, *95*
trance, shamans in, 92
trance (medicine) dance of Bushmen, 26, *26–7*, 28–9
Trans-Amazonian highway, *128*
traps: for fish, 40; for land animals, 38
trees: Barama River Caribs and spirits of, 58; children identified with, 56; *see also* forests
truffles, 44
Tsembaga people (New Guinea), swidden cultivators, 49, 71
Tukano people (Peru), *68*, *69*
Turkana people (Kenya): camel-herding by, *54–5*; fishing by, *40–1*
turtle ceremony, in puberty rite of Andaman Islanders, 117

U nemployment, of Indians in U.S.A., 120
United Nations Conference on Human Environment (1972), 137
United States of America, Indians in, 120–6
urban man: aberrations of, 29–30; fishing by, 38; food gathering by, 43–4; hunting by, 36; and natural man, 118–39

V enezuela, Amerindians of, *38*
Villas-Boas, Claudio and Orlando, *130*, 131, *131*, *132*, *133*, *139*
violence: avoidance of, 25, 80–1; ritualization of, 78, 82, *82*, 83; senseless, a recent aberration? 30; society of urban man fascinated by, 78
"violin," of Bushmen, *98*

W alruses, *62–3*
war game, of Chimbu people, *82*
Waura Indians (Brazil): fishing, *43*, mother and child, *101*
wealth, prestige from, 100
whales, hunted by Eskimos, 38
Wikmunkan people (Australia), totems of, 60
wild rice, harvested by Chippewa Indians, 44, *44*, 45
wildebeest, *16*
women: as cooks, *105*; as gardeners, 50, *50–1*; not to approach salmon fisheries, 40; not to see Kamayura sacred flutes, *93*; as pig-keepers, 53; as plant gatherers, 20, *22*, 23; polygamy justified by economic importance of, 45–6
Worimi tribe (Australia), sex totems in, 95
Wounded Knee, U.S.A.: Second Battle of (1973), *124*, *125*; tragedy of (1890), *124*
wrestling, among Amerindians, *83*

X avante people (Brazil): health of, 73; remnant of, 128
Xingu National Park, Brazil, 131, *138–9*

Y ankton Sioux (South Dakota), factory set up by, 133–4
Yanomamo people (Venezuela), health of, 73, 110
Yaqui people (North Mexico), shaman of, 92

Picture Credits

Key to position of picture on page: (B) bottom, (C) center, (L) left, (R) right, (T) top; hence (BR) bottom right, (CL) center left, etc.

Cover: Robin Smith/The Photographic Library of Australia
Title page: T. Eigeland/Black Star, New York
Contents: *Daily Telegraph* Color Library
8 Ed Drews/Photo Researchers
9(R) David Moore/Black Star, New York
10 Jen & Des Bartlett/Bruce Coleman Ltd.
11(B) National Museum of Kenya, courtesy Mr. Richard Leakey
14(L) Tony Carr/Colorific!
15 Fred Bruemmer
16 Gerald Cubitt
17 Brian Seed/Magnum Photos
18–20 Irven DeVore
21 Dieter Heunemann, Max-Planck-Institut, Percha
22 P. Jaunet/Aspect
23 Irven DeVore
24(B) Irven DeVore
25 Laurence K. Marshall
26–7 Irven DeVore
28(L) © Commander Gatti Expeditions
29 Picturepoint, London
31 Gerald Cubitt
32(BL) Information Canada Photothèque
32(CB) E. Hummel/ZEFA
32(BR) Donald McCullin and *Sunday Times Magazine*
33(BL) P. Jaunot/Aspect
33(CB) Irven DeVore
33(BR) Colorofic!
34(L) J. Launois/Black Star, New York
35(L) David Moore/Black Star, New York
35(R) Document Henri Lhote's expedition
37(T) © Commander Gatti Expeditions
37(B) Dieter Heunemann, Max-Planck-Institut, Percha
38 Jacques Jangoux/Photo Researchers
39 J. Allan Cash Ltd.
41 Photo Mirella Ricciardi from *Vanishing Africa,* Collins Publishers, London
42 Stan Wayman/Photo Researchers
43 Vilma Chiara Schultz
44–5 Robert Jarvenpa, Department of Anthropology, State University of New York at Albany
46(L) Vilma Chiara Schultz
47 Axel Poignant
48–51 Vilma Chiara Schultz
52 Th. Franz/ZEFA
53(R) Photo Mirella Ricciardi from *Vanishing Africa,* Collins Publishers, London
54–5 Photo Mirella Ricciardi from *Vanishing Africa,* Collins Publishers, London
56 R. Barry Ranfored/Transworld
57(TR) *Daily Telegraph* Color Library
57(B) Education Development Center, Newton, Mass.
59 Jacques Jangoux/Photo Researchers
60 James Fitzpatrick/The Photographic Library of Australia
61(TR) Axel Poignant
61(BR) Fritz Goro, *Epic of Man,* 1962 © Time Inc. 1973
62–3(B) Education Development Center, Newton, Mass.
63(T) Fred Bruemmer
64 Irven DeVore
65(T) Dieter Heunemann, Max-Planck-Institut, Percha
65(B) Gordon Gahian/Photo Researchers
68 Brian Moser
69(TL, B) Brian Moser
69(TR) Photo Researchers
70(B) Vilma Chiara Schultz
71 John Moss/Colorific!
72 Irven DeVore
73 David Moore/Colorific!
74–5 John Nance/Magnum Photos
77 Photo Josef Muench
78–9 Axel Poignant
80 Photos Professor Klaus-Friedrich Koch
81–2 Axel Poignant
83 Vilma Chiara Schultz
85 Courtesy of Kennedy Galleries, Inc.
86–7 George Rodger/Magnum Photos
88 Vilma Chiara Schultz
90–1 Photos Josef Muench
92(BL) Robin Hanbury Tenison/Robert Harding Associates
92(TR, B) Vilma Chiara Schultz
93 Donald McCullin and *Sunday Times Magazine*
94 Doug Wilson/Black Star, New York
95 Axel Poignant
96 Irven DeVore
97(L) Victor Englebert/Transworld
97(R) Laurence K. Marshall
98(T) Dieter Heunemann, Max-Planck-Institut, Percha
98(B) Robin Hanbury Tenison/Robert Harding Associates
99 Vilma Chiara Schultz
100–3 Axel Poignant
104–5 Brian Moser
106–7 John Nance/Magnum Photos
109 Tony Carr/Colorific!
110 Vilma Chiara Schultz
111 Irven DeVore
112 Robin Smith/The Photographic Library of Australia
113(TR) David Moore/Colorific!
113(BR) N. Tucker/Photo Researchers
114(B) Axel Poignant
115(T) David Moore/Transworld
115(B) Photo Professor Klaus-Friedrich Koch
116 John Moss/Colorific!
117 Photos Professor Klaus-Friedrich Koch
118–9 Richard Erdoes/Gamma
120–1 Fred Bruemmer
122 Picturepoint, London
123(R) Robert Jarvenpa, Department of Anthropology, State University of New York at Albany
124–7 Richard Erdoes/Gamma
128 Donald McCullin and *Sunday Times Magazine*
129 John Dominis, *Life* 71 © Time Inc.
130 Adrian Cowells/Transworld
132(TL) Adrian Cowells/Transworld
132(B) Vilma Chiara Schultz
133 Vilma Chiara Schultz
134 FPG
135 David Moore/Black Star, New York
136 Tony Carr/Colorific!
139 John Moss/Colorific!

Artist Credits

© Aldus Books: Amaryllis May 11; David Nockels 12, 32–3, 66–7